# normal

# normal

*a mother and
her beautiful son*

Magdalena Newman

with Hilary Liftin

Houghton Mifflin Harcourt
Boston   New York
2020

For information about permission to reproduce selections from this book,
write to trade.permissions@hmhco.com or to Permissions,
Houghton Mifflin Harcourt Publishing Company, 3 Park Avenue,
19th Floor, New York, New York 10016.

hmhbooks.com

*Library of Congress Cataloging-in-Publication Data*
Names: Newman, Magdalena M., author. | Liftin, Hilary, author.
Title: Normal : a mother and her beautiful son / Magdalena Newman ;
with Hilary Liftin.
Description: Boston ; New York : Houghton Mifflin Harcourt, 2020.
Identifiers: LCCN 2019023276 (print) | LCCN 2019023277 (ebook) |
ISBN 9781328593122 (hardback) | ISBN 9780358172260 | ISBN
9780358306702 | ISBN 9781328592354 (ebook)
Subjects: LCSH: Facial bones—Abnormalities—Biography. |
Newman, Nathaniel. | Newman, Magdalena M. | Genetic disorders—
Biography. | Mothers and sons. | Families—Washington (State)—Seattle. |
Seattle (Wash.)—Biography.
Classification: LCC QM695.F32 N49 2020b (print) |
LCC QM695.F32 (ebook) | DDC 611/.716—dc23
LC record available at https://lccn.loc.gov/2019023276
LC ebook record available at https://lccn.loc.gov/2019023277

Book design by Carly Miller

Printed in the United States of America
DOC 10 9 8 7 6 5 4 3 2 1

# contents

# foreword by r.j. palacio, author of *wonder*

I first met Magda over lunch on Carmine Street, near my office. *Wonder* had just come out the month before. My book about a boy with a facial difference and the community around him was holding its own in the marketplace, sales-wise, which was a bit of a surprise to everyone—especially me—given that it was a debut book by a first-time author. Moreover, friends confessed that they themselves had put off reading it because they assumed it would be "a downer." So when *Wonder* started getting out in the world, finding an audience, it felt a little miraculous to me. More miraculous, though, were the emails and letters I started receiving from people within the craniofacial community. Children who looked like Auggie, or had other types of facial syndromes, their parents and siblings and grandparents, their doctors and nurses, started writing to me about the positive impact the book was having on their lives.

Of all of these emails, the one I remember the most vividly is the email that came from Russel Newman via a nurse who we both knew at the NYU Medical Center. I remember it well because he sent me a picture of Nathaniel, and the moment I saw

Nathaniel's face, I thought to myself: That is exactly how I pictured Auggie Pullman.

In those days, there weren't enough people requesting to meet me that I couldn't comply, quite happily, with their request. So when Russel asked to meet me for lunch, I said sure!

I was already sitting in the restaurant when they arrived. The first thing I could not help but note was how beautiful Magda was. Treacher Collins is often hereditary, and by then I'd met many families in which a mom or dad had discovered they themselves had a mild form of TCS after the birth of a child with a more severe form of it. (One dad once joked, "I just thought I was funny-looking, that's all!") But neither Russel nor Magda had any trace of the syndrome and, in fact, looked like they had walked out of the pages of a magazine. The second thing I noted was that Magda was walking with the help of a walker, which seemed at odds with her very athletic frame. I assumed it was a sports injury. It was not.

In the course of that lunch, which was one of the most memorable in my life, I came to learn all about the Newman family. I learned, while both laughing and crying, about the journey that had brought them to this moment, stories that you are about to read. I learned about their courtship, and the birth of their first son, Nathaniel, whose Treacher Collins syndrome was a complete surprise to them, discovered on the day he was born. I learned what it was like for them as they took in the enormity of Nathaniel's condition that first night of his life, having had no time to prepare or research, as they dealt with both the immediate challenges of having a newborn whose odds of surviving the night were slim, and the long-term challenges that his physical condition would bring. I learned about the many surgeries Nathaniel went through, and about the toll this often took on their family—

and on their younger son, Jacob, especially—and the heartbreak and stress it brought . . . but also about the unexpected joys. I learned that they were ordinary people who were dealing, as best they could, with the extraordinary lives they had been given. I learned that they were funny and warm and incredibly kind, and that Russel cried easily and Magda smiled easily.

I feel so blessed to be friends with Magda. I feel like I am a better person by knowing her. I am stronger. I am wiser. To say that she is an inspiration is not enough, because it's so much more than that. She is everything I would hope to be if ever faced with the challenges and choices she has had to deal with in life. She is the measure against which I hold myself.

I am so glad she is sharing her story with the world, that others might learn what I've learned from having seen this "unsinkable Molly Brown" rise again and again whenever life knocks her down: that, no matter what, you just get back up.

Like the wise words in Natalie Merchant's song "Wonder," Magda is that person who, "with love, with patience, and with faith" will "make her way." And blaze a path for the rest of us while doing it.

*A normal life. A normal family.*
*What is normal?*
*Maybe normal is what is most common.*
*Maybe normal is what is least noticeable.*
*Maybe normal is a judgment coming from someone else.*
*Maybe normal is your own imagined ideal.*
*Where is the line between normal and not-normal?*
*Who gets to decide?*

*part one*

# a beautiful baby boy

# 1. beautiful

*Nathaniel: In summer of 2017 when we got to Beaver Lake, I ran straight into the water. I was wearing a big Spider-Man floaty—but only because it was a very deep lake. I paddled out as far as I could as fast as I could, singing to myself, "Don't stop believing you can do this." When my parents tell this story, it sounds like I was having a deep, spiritual moment, but in truth I was joking around, trying to swim to my mom, and wondering how far I could go.*

*When I got to what felt like the middle of the lake, I floated on my back, spreading out my arms and legs like a starfish, looking up at the blue sky. I was alone, truly alone. Nobody watching would have noticed me and thought, "Hey, that kid is alone." After all, there were plenty of other people in the lake and I knew three of them. My mother was on a paddleboard. My brother and father were somewhere behind me. But, as far as I was concerned, I was alone, and today was not an ordinary day.*

*We've gone swimming as a family plenty of times. My dad*

used to be a lifeguard, so he loves to swim. I've watched him throw my brother, Jacob, in various pools and bodies of water for as long as I can remember. And countless times Jacob has cannonballed into the water right near me just to irritate my mother. Whenever we went to a pool or a lake, my mother, who never really learned to swim right, hovered near me in the shallow end, keeping the coast clear of splashy toddlers and annoying younger brothers. Every single time I went swimming, up until this day, I had to wear water wings on my hands and feet and a life preserver around my stomach to keep my head as far above the surface as possible. Even doggy-paddling would have put my neck dangerously close to the water. Water, in this situation, was my kryptonite.

But on this day, for the first time ever, the embarrassing flotation devices were gone. My mother was giving me space. For a good distance, all around me, there was only the flat lake. It was amazing and ordinary at the same time.

I was thirteen years old, and I had never been able to swim by myself. I had put my head under water a few times, just for a few seconds, but that was completely against the doctors' orders. Now, sixty-seven surgeries later, I could finally swim like normal kids, without the flotation devices bobbling around me, without an adult ready to help me if something went wrong.

If you looked at it from the outside, I had worked really hard for this moment: having operations to help me breathe, recovering, getting used to a new normal, then doing the whole thing all over again many times. But the surgeries didn't feel like achievements I deserved applause for—I'd been having surgeries ever since I was born. What I felt in Beaver Lake wasn't a sense of accomplishment, but a new level of independence. Like a first ride on the school bus. A sleepover. What

*I imagine it will feel like when I can finally drive a car. I'd wanted to swim by myself for so long it was hard to believe it was actually real. Though my brain was still processing the change, the water was energizing. The sky was wide open. The whole world stretched around me. I felt free.*

It is hard to describe how I felt watching my son swim for the first time or what it represented for our family. Nathaniel had never been alone. It may not seem like such a big deal—thirteen is still young—but before that day at Beaver Lake, Nathaniel had never been in water more than a few feet from an adult, not in his entire life, and getting him there had been my full-time job.

Before Nathaniel was born, his father and I were a typical young couple. Russel and I lived in a small apartment on the Upper East Side of Manhattan until I got pregnant and we moved across the river to Hoboken, New Jersey, where you could get more space—how perfectly normal. At the time, I was writing my thesis to earn my masters in music theory and composition at a music academy in Gdansk, Poland, where I was born. To help make ends meet, I also worked at a friend's boutique, selling jeans. Russel was just getting started as an insurance underwriter at Chubb. We had decent health coverage, and I had a good doctor. I was twenty-four and healthy.

There was no reason to worry, no reason to do any special tests. At my six-month sonogram the doctor said, "His nose looks big," and was surprised that my amniotic fluid seemed to be building up, but assured us there was no reason for real concern.

I went into labor right on time and was pretty far along when Russel and I arrived at the hospital. My doctor smiled at me and said, "Do you want to hold your baby when he's born?"

"Of course I do! Yes!" I replied.

• • •

In addition to Russel, there were a couple nurses in the room and, because it was a teaching hospital, there were also some students. Sunshine poured through the windows, brightening the delivery room after a long night of labor, and the sheets below me felt crisp and sterile. This was finally happening. A baby! As the doctor delivered Nathaniel, Russel stood beside him, wearing scrubs and cheering me on, saying, "Oh my God, you've got this! I see the head! He's got dark hair." Then, all of a sudden, a mask dropped over Russel's excited face. His mouth opened in a silent wail, his eyes got huge, and he went white. He grabbed his hair and started pulling it. At the same time, a horrible smell entered the room. I waited to hear the cry of a newborn but instead, I saw every single person's face change to the same mask of pure shock.

They hurried a bundle off to a little alcove connected to the delivery room. Russel followed.

"What's going on?" I asked. "Where's my baby?"

Then I heard Russel wailing, "Oh God, oh my God!"

"Is the baby alive?" I asked the suddenly hushed room. There was a quiet rush of activity off to the side where I could barely see them. Nobody answered me. "Is the baby alive?" I was shaking now, confused and terrified. What was happening? The silent baby, that dreadful smell, Russel's howls. My doctor was still tending to me, finishing up his work with his head down, but otherwise nobody was paying attention to me. Nobody would even look at me.

Finally my doctor said, "Yes, he's alive."

Nobody offered to let me hold him or see him. Nothing. They seemed scared to show me my son. From the corner of my eye I could see into the room where they were cleaning him, and when they lifted him up for a moment, I caught a glimpse of a cone-shaped head and eyes that looked big and swollen. It had been a rough birth, I told myself, maybe that was all. . . . I caught a glimpse of one ear. It didn't look like a normal ear. Then I saw his profile. It wasn't just his ear—something was very wrong.

"Did I deliver an alien?" I asked my doctor. "Is that a child? What happened? What happened?"

"He has issues. Let's see if he's stable."

Five minutes passed. The room stayed strangely quiet. The baby still wasn't crying. I had the sense that they were working on him, but I wasn't even sure he was still alive.

Lying on the bed in the delivery room, the only thing I could think to do was call my mother, who was waiting for news of our baby boy. I asked for a phone and someone gave me one. My mother answered. I could picture her back in our house in Sanok, a small town in southeast Poland, the last real town in the Bieszczady Mountains before civilization fades to tiny villages. I knew exactly where she had to be standing, using the only phone we'd ever had, still attached to the living room wall in the house where I'd grown up. The room was full of generic Communist furniture, crowded with tchotchkes like glass fish and tiny shot glasses, my father's sculptures, and religious icons—treasures that told a simple story of faith and love and family.

"I don't know what happened, Mom, but I think I delivered an alien."

She asked what I was talking about.

"Mom, it doesn't have an ear. I'm a musician. How can I have a baby with no ear?" What kind of terrible person calls her own baby an alien, an "it"? All I can say is that I was not myself.

Without missing a beat, my mother said that as long as the baby had two arms, two legs, and a head, everything would be okay. Those were the only things that mattered. It helped a little, somehow, to hear her soothing, maternal tones. I tried to breathe. I still hadn't seen my son, and now he was no longer in the room.

"We don't know what's wrong, but the baby's face is severely deformed," Russel told me.

"Deformed" is a word that doctors use, though many people dislike it. But at that point we were still oblivious to such details. I was in a recovery room—at least I thought that was where I was—but I wasn't sure whether what was happening was real or a nightmare. A fog of emotions and medication brought me in and out of consciousness; I was shaking, fainting, delirious. Had I given birth or imagined it? Was what I'd seen real? No, I never had the baby I'd had a glimpse of, a baby with a condition I'd never heard of, never seen, never even known to pray it wouldn't be part of my story. I'd read *What to Expect When You're Expecting* twice, once in English and once in Polish, and I was quite certain there hadn't been anything to prepare me for this. No, I was still pregnant and everything was fine. Somebody would wake me up from this dream.

This invention. This nightmare.

At last a team of doctors, all with unfamiliar faces, came to address me. They handed me a book from the 1970s open to a dated picture of a person with droopy eyes, a severely small jaw, and a distinctive bird-like look.

"Your son has Treacher Collins syndrome. It's a congenital disorder. He has craniofacial deformities—his ears, eye sockets, cheekbones, jawbone—they haven't formed normally," one of the doctors explained.

I was devastated. I didn't want my child to look like this picture. I didn't ask if he was going to be okay, if he would have a normal life span, or if he would be mentally disabled. The outside was enough to worry about. It was too much already.

Another doctor said, "He will be physically challenged. He has almost no jaw. He can't hear. He's having trouble breathing."

Russel reappeared from checking on the baby. Russel, who was always calm, who always knew what to do, who was the guy you wanted in an emergency, had a look of panic in his eyes that I'd never seen before. He put a hand on my shoulder, gripping me tightly, and said, "It's severe. It's real."

Night passed into morning. My in-laws arrived: Russel's parents and his brothers and their wives. But instead of it being a happy moment, everyone who visited was crying as though someone had died. The baby was alive, with a future ahead of him, but none of us could imagine what that future looked like. It certainly wasn't going to be what any of us had expected. Our distress was so loud that they moved us to a private area. I think we were scaring the other expectant and new parents.

It's hard to say this now, but I had bad thoughts. It crossed my mind that maybe it would be better if the baby died. How could he live like this? Live *through* this? Could I hold him? Could I love him? How could I take care of him? Why was this happening to me? Why did God punish me?

Most of that first day is a blur. I remember Russel on the chair next to my bed. He is unshaven, dark circles under his eyes, his hair a mess. He shakes his head, crying. I am only half-present, drifting into oblivion only to open my eyes to the same nightmare. When I come to, Russel asks me if I want to go see him.

I say no. I'm not ready. I'm scared.

He's breathing, Russel tells me. He's with the preemies, and they gave him a tiny preemie bassinette. He's so long that his legs are sticking out of it. He's fighting for every breath.

The TV was on in the recovery room, a strange tether to the outside world, a world that continued forward despite our tortured confusion. As Russel wept, I prayed. *This is the worst day of my life. Give me strength. Give me a sign. Give me something to hold on to.*

It was February 8, 2004, and the Grammys were on. Christina Aguilera came onscreen. She walked onto an empty, round platform, dressed simply in a dark suit, with bare feet and dark hair. She sang: "We're beautiful in every single way. Yes, words won't bring us down . . ."

Russel and I stared at each other in absolute amazement. It was like she was speaking directly to us. Her words didn't solve any of Nathaniel's medical issues, but they answered all the questions and fears that were circling in my head. In that moment, I felt something physically change — a weird strength rose in me. It was almost like I felt God's presence. He had given me a sign. No matter how my child looked, he would be beautiful. I had been chosen to be his mother. I would love him — I already did. I always had.

Right then, as we listened to the song, I promised God that I would do everything I possibly could to treat our child as a beautiful soul, a beautiful spirit, a beautiful human.

Russel was holding my hand. He said, "Magda, this is going to be our beautiful child no matter what happens. He's going to change the world one day."

We both cried, though my tears were different now, no longer tears of fear but of possibility. I was going to turn this situation around and create the best possible outcome. Every parent hopes and believes his child will change the world. Russel and I had the same hope, except that before Nathaniel started making the world a better place, we needed him to live.

I got out of the bed, put on a white robe from Victoria's Secret that Russel had brought me—a robe that had been meant to welcome a healthy infant, a leftover gift from another lifetime. That didn't matter anymore. I didn't look back at the plans we'd made in blissful ignorance. We were on a new path. We walked to the nursery where our baby was resting alongside the preemies. I was ready for him.

We named our son Nathaniel. Later, at his bris, when it came time to pick a Hebrew name for him, our rabbi said, "You don't have to choose another name. 'Nathaniel' is already a Hebrew name. It means 'gift from God.'"

It would be a while before I reached in the pocket of an old coat and found a little notebook that I had once used for addresses, train schedules, recipes, and odd notes. Written in it was a list that Russel and I had come up with several years before, when we first met. Sitting at a cafe in Prague, fantasizing about our future family, we had scribbled down a few baby names, and for a boy, we had written Nathaniel and Jakub (the Polish form of Jacob).

Long before our special boy was born, we had somehow anticipated our gift from God.

*Nathaniel: When I was born, I could hardly breathe. My nose didn't connect to my airway, and because my jaw was so small, my tongue filled my mouth. There were problems with most of my senses. I couldn't smell because my cheekbones were behind my nose, blocking it. I couldn't eat because my jaw was small and out of alignment. I could barely hear because I didn't have ears to capture the sound and deliver it to my brain.*

*I didn't have bottom eyelids, which meant I couldn't close my eyes fully, and my vision wasn't great, although that was just run-of-the-mill bad luck. Bonus! The only good news on my five senses report card was that I could feel—everything about me from the neck down worked just fine. And my brain was perfectly fine too, maybe even a little bit awesome, if I do say so myself, which would help me deal with all the other problems.*

*I grew up knowing that I had Treacher Collins and that it made me different, but I didn't feel different. I felt like myself, the only self I'd ever known. Other kids weren't fed through a tube in their stomach for the first year and a half of their lives. Other kids didn't wear hearing aids. Other kids didn't have a hole in their neck to help them breathe. Other kids didn't grow up having doctors' appointments instead of soccer practice and surgeries instead of vacations. Other kids didn't have a nurse with them at school. Other kids could shower, swim, play roughly, go out in the rain.*

*The way I see it, a certain number of kids are going to be born with issues like mine every year—an estimated 1 in 50,000, if you ask the people who count. That's not very many, but that's just the kids with Treacher Collins. Every year, tens of thousands of kids are born with facial differences in North America, and plenty more have other, different problems to deal with. I definitely don't want to do the math on that, but I know that if you add all those kids together, I'm just one in a huge crowd. If you look at it that way, I'm pretty normal after all.*

In February of 2012 the book *Wonder* by R.J. Palacio was published. *Wonder* is the story of Auggie Pullman, a boy with a craniofacial condition that is called mandibulofacial dysostosis in the book, another name for Treacher Collins. Our family cannot overstate the effect this book has had on our lives. Nathaniel had just turned eight when it was published, and it immediately transformed the way people saw and approached him in playgrounds, at school, in the world. Auggie won the hearts of readers, and it's not an exaggeration to say that his story taught a whole generation of children, and many to follow, to accept others who look different and to choose kindness. This was life-changing—*Wonder* introduced the rest of the world to some of what we had been dealing with throughout Nathaniel's whole life, and, in doing so, helped readers feel true empathy for real people living with facial differences, or *any* differences!

R.J. was inspired to write *Wonder* by her son's reactions to a little girl in their neighborhood who had Treacher Collins, and the book focuses on the sociopsychological aspects of Auggie's experiences—the challenges he faces interacting with the people around him. For us, the way people treat Nathaniel, how they see him, and what he looks like do matter—probably to me more than him—but the social component was eclipsed by the physical challenges he faced on a daily basis from the moment he was born. Normal was our goal, but for us "normal" wasn't about what Nathaniel saw in the mirror or how kids treated him. "Normal" meant seeing, eating, hearing, breathing. Normal was a happy, carefree childhood.

Who is to say what constitutes "normal"? When you call the thing that is most common normal, you are suggesting that there is something abnormal, wrong, or even *bad* about being different—there is judgment in the word. And in the beginning, when I yearned for normal, part of what I wanted was not just for Nathaniel to have the comfort and opportunities that any other kid would take for granted, but also for him to be freed from that judgment.

My destiny was to raise a child who was born deaf, unable to eat or close his eyes, and barely able to breathe. A child who lived in a world where every sense was a hard-won victory. A world in which only science and love make anything possible.

## 2. congratulations

Even the nurses were scared when I first walked into the NICU (neonatal intensive care unit) nursery. I felt like I was about to deliver a speech or have the most important job interview of my life. In a strange way, it was a feeling I recognized from stepping on stage to perform a piano concert back in Poland. I was scared and sweating, but I remembered how to take a deep breath and rise to the challenge.

The first thing I saw were those long legs, poking out over the end of the bassinet. Russel was right—our boy was too long for the preemie bassinet. Then I saw his little face with big, big eyes. He was gasping for air and, although he was almost a day old, he hadn't had anything to eat yet because he couldn't suck. But somehow, inconceivably, he seemed to be smiling at me. Picking him up for the first time, I held him in my arms and said, "I love you, I love you," half to reassure myself that I did love him. Then I looked him in the eyes and saw the tiny human in there wanting to survive, wanting to live. My baby. Gazing at him, I thought, "You're my soulmate now. I'm going to protect you and make sure you're okay. I'll provide anything you need."

The doctors and nurses who were taking care of Nathaniel

were getting nervous about the fact that this baby hadn't eaten. He couldn't nurse or take a bottle. He choked on formula when they tried giving it to him from a syringe. He had the instinct to suck—he'd try, making little sucking noises—but physically he just couldn't do it. His jaw was so tiny that his tongue, which was unaffected by Treacher Collins, was too big for his mouth. He would cough as he tried to breathe and swallow at the same time. Finally they put a feeding catheter down his throat. It wasn't a long-term solution, but they didn't seem to know what else to do.

Where should we take the baby to get him help? Who would know what was wrong with him and how to deal with it? Russel is a man of action. That first day he started calling people: every doctor we knew, every person we knew who might know a doctor, every person we knew who might know a person who might know a doctor. In a crisis, Russel's mind is sharp and efficient, and by that night he announced, "NYU has a bed for our son. There's a team of doctors there specializing in Treacher Collins."

Though I had never heard of, much less worried about, this syndrome, it turned out it wasn't as rare as I had assumed—one in 50,000 babies is born with it, to varying degrees. Nathaniel was severely affected—there was no prognosis for his immediate survival, much less his quality of life going forward, but knowing that there was a group of doctors who were devoted to helping babies like him was immensely reassuring. Help existed.

The next morning the nurses wrapped Nathaniel up like a burrito and we headed across town in an ambulance to NYU Medical Center. On the ride there, I watched every breath he took.

When we arrived at the craniofacial ward at NYU, we were greeted at the door by a woman who introduced herself as Shelley Cohen. She was the speech pathologist who happened to have been on call when Russel phoned the hospital the night before. She'd arranged for the transfer and had been waiting for us to arrive.

Shelley came up to me, smiled into the bundle I was carrying, and said, "Congratulations, you have a beautiful baby boy."

It was the first time anyone had congratulated me on the birth of my son. In that moment I absorbed how different my experience was from that of most new mothers, but at the same time, Shelley's kind words gave me hope that they would come true. My baby could stabilize. He would eat, breathe, and smile. And most important, he would live. I finally felt there was a way for us to move closer to "normal," to climb out of this nightmare and live as parents and child, in a home, not a hospital, eating meals as a family. What had seemed like a given before Nathaniel was born was now, at least, a possibility.

Nathaniel had two surgeries in the next forty-eight hours. Now that he's had sixty-seven surgeries I can say that kind of casually, but at the time the notion of someone operating on our tiny child was terrifying, even knowing how badly he needed help.

The first thing they did was put in a gastrointestinal tube. This "g-tube" would allow him to be fed directly into his stomach until the doctors found a way for him to use his mouth. They told me he would be much more comfortable without the catheter in his throat, so although it wasn't a solution, it was an improvement.

The second not-to-be-discussed-over-dinner surgery was to drill a hole in the bone that was blocking his airway. He was only breathing through his tiny mouth, and this would let him use his nose. Or so we hoped. Our naïveté protected us from what was to come.

When the craniofacial team at NYU stabilized Nathaniel — allowing him to take in air and nutrients — it had the side effect of stabilizing me. The fog of fear and confusion lifted and I began to see our situation in more practical terms. Nathaniel would need help with life functions, which would require multiple surgeries and prolonged medical attention. It would require all of our resources: every bit of strength and faith, all of our time and energy, every dime we had. He would struggle physically, but, like almost all people with Treacher Collins, he was unaffected mentally.

This was the first time I stopped to realize that behind his face, which cried out for help and repair, was a curious little mind, ready to greet the world. My child would recognize me and love me! And he would learn about butterflies, get lost in books, and explore the world, even if often from a hospital bed. The good — great — saving grace was that I would be able to bond with him, so I began to focus on that. Besides, now that I had held him, all the maternal hormones had kicked in. We were already connected, and I was determined to make his world warm and safe. Determined . . . but crying. Those maternal hormones had a bonus feature: shock and trauma gave way to the worry of boundless love. This child was everything to me, and I couldn't stop crying.

Russel comforted me, never questioning my ability to be Nathaniel's mother. He knew I was exhausted and realized that my simple, hardworking life before had in no way prepared me for this experience. But he always says it was Nathaniel's spirit that gave me strength. He tells Nathaniel, "The picture I have in my mind is your mother sitting in a rocking chair in the NICU. She is clutching you to her chest. Tubes are springing out of you in every direction, but your mom is humming, caressing you, loving you."

# 3. the first twenty-eight days

The NICU became our new home. There were eight cribs, eight preemies, all small, sweet versions of what you expect a baby to look like. Nathaniel looked enormous next to them. His issues were more obvious than theirs, but his prognosis was better. Some of the preemies were at much higher risk, whereas now that he was stable, he would definitely make it out of this hospital. Like us, most of the families there had expected to bring home a healthy child.

Every family with a baby in the NICU, and later the PICU (pediatric intensive care unit), had their own story of fear, anxiety, and heartbreak. For the most part we were all so focused on our own children that we lived our vigils in parallel isolation, but sometimes I had a glimpse into another mother's world.

There was a room where every new mom would sit to pump breast milk for the babies who couldn't suck. When we were done, we put it in a special refrigerator where we had shelves labeled with our names. Some of the mothers who couldn't stay at the hospital pumped at home and brought in milk that the nurses could feed their babies when they weren't there.

Nathaniel's milk shelf was labeled "N. Newman." The shelf above it was labeled "Neuman" and was used by a Hasidic mother, a sweet woman who was always kind to me. She and her husband often prayed, and once she gave me a small bible. She told me that, according to tradition, their baby wouldn't be named until it came home.

One day there was a commotion outside the NICU and the nurses came in to find me. Apparently they had given baby Neuman a full night's worth of the breast milk that I had pumped for Nathaniel.

The Hasidic family was distraught. The father asked me a number of questions about my culture and practices. He wanted to know my diet and whether I ate pork.

"I'm from Poland," I said. "I'm sorry. But my husband is Jewish?"

This didn't appease them. Russel wasn't considered Jewish in their culture. The father was so upset he couldn't look me in the eye.

The nurses apologetically asked if they could take my blood so they could reassure the family that the baby hadn't been exposed to anything. I gave them about six vials. Baby Neuman was fine, but I think one of the nurses lost her job that morning.

There was another baby, a dark-haired girl who lay still in her bassinet. She was intubated and gave no signs of life. When the mother, who looked about fifteen years old, visited, she'd put the baby in pretty dresses and play with her like she was a doll. I never saw the father.

When I finally asked the nurses, who had become my friends, about this young mother, they told me, "The baby is brain dead. The dad shook her, and she won't recover from the brain trauma. If they take her off life support, the baby will die and the father will go to prison. They're waiting for his trial."

The doctors were trying to convince them it was time to turn off the machines, but the family refused.

In the hallway outside the NICU they had photos of babies who had spent time in the hospital. A year later I came in for an appointment and went to say hello to the nurses. I noticed that there was a photo of that young mother holding her baby— but the girl was much bigger. She must have been eight months old, and she was still hooked up to the life-support machines. I have no idea how long they kept that baby in that state, but it was heartbreaking. All these parents, sharing the same pain, but trapped in their own tragedies.

There was another family I would meet later, when Nathaniel was in the PICU, which was across the hall from the NICU and would itself become another home away from home. The mother had two boys, who were five and seven. The younger son was very sick. There was something wrong with his heart, and he had been in the hospital for four months. Russel and I would hang out with the seven-year-old, who was very cute and chatty.

One day I went home for a couple of hours to shower, and when I returned, the five-year-old boy's bed was empty. All of the cards, photos, and stuffed animals that had decorated his area were gone. The whole family was there, and his mother said to me, "Come see him."

She led me down the hallway into a room I'd never been in before, a rarely used chapel where they brought the little ones who didn't make it. "Look how peaceful he is," she said. She was right. It was the first time I'd seen him free from tubes and machines, and he looked like he was smiling.

His older brother said, "I never saw him sleeping like that. He was always in pain." That was an eye-opening moment for me. I could not pity myself for being in the hospital with my baby because, at the end of the ordeal, I would get to go home with him. My son was going to be okay. I would focus on the miracle that we had, not the challenges that went with it.

## 4. to eat

I was scared to bring Nathaniel home. In the hospital a whole team of specialists watched over him, and they took care of me too, making sure I showered and ate. They had come to feel like family.

Before any parent leaves the hospital with a new baby, there is what seems to be a mandatory check to confirm that they have a properly installed car seat and know how to strap the baby in safely. Our discharge involved training in a special form of CPR, learning how to clean the g-tube and care for the skin around it, and making sure that we knew what supplies to have on hand and how to order new ones.

When parents leave the hospital with a newborn, they often take a photo, capturing the moment: *This is us leaving the hospital. This is us taking responsibility for our own small, vulnerable creature.* You can usually see a bit of nervous anticipation mixed with the joy in their eyes. When we were discharged from the hospital, to say we were nervous was an understatement. Nathaniel was twenty-eight days old, his life especially fragile. And it was all completely foreign. We'd had no examples of the kind of parenting we were supposed to do, not by our friends and families or in any movie or TV show.

Our little apartment in Hoboken was only two rooms, so during my final trimester we'd set up a crib in our bedroom. We'd picked a set of Winnie-the-Pooh sheets, and they came with a couple of pictures of Winnie-the-Pooh that I'd hung on the wall next to the crib. Russel's brother Hal and his wife, Nancy, had thrown a baby shower for us at their house in Long Island. I still didn't know many people in New York, so it was just Russel's family, some friends of his from work, and my cousin. We hadn't registered for gifts, but they'd given us toys and clothes, tiny white clothes that I'd carefully organized in a dresser with a changing station on top.

The first time I'd come home from the hospital to shower and get new clothes, I'd noted the empty crib, waiting expectantly for the baby who wasn't healthy enough to sleep in it. The crib itself looked as innocent as we had been, so simple and steady in its belief that a baby would soon rest in its arms. How long would it wait, I wondered? How long would it be before my baby was detached from the machines that made it hard to cuddle him?

That moment had finally arrived. It was almost a month later than we'd expected when I rested Nathaniel in his crib, though a few changes had been made. Instead of the sweet, calm nest where I'd envisioned nursing him and singing lullabies, the room was surrounded by equipment, like a hospital room. There were tall poles from which feeding bags hung, and boxes of extra bags and baby formula filled the room.

During the time we'd been at the hospital, Nathaniel had already outgrown most of the newborn clothes in the dresser, and the ones that might have fit, he couldn't wear. I cleared them out to make room for clothes with buttons in the front so we could easily access his g-tube.

Bringing a new baby home is always an adjustment. Taking care of this baby was going to be more complicated than feeding, burping, and the occasional diaper blowout. Nathaniel's g-tube looked like an extra belly button, and for now it was the only way he could eat. But he had trouble keeping formula down, and "trouble" is an understatement. You know how things start hurting more after you leave the doctor's office? Well, pretty much as soon as we got home, Nathaniel started throwing up everything he ate. There was a pump to continuously drip food through the g-tube. Instead of taking in formula through his mouth down to his stomach, it was the other way around. He threw up as I fed him. I dragged our ruined carpets out to the curb, resterilized the equipment, and tried again and again, desperate for him to keep anything down.

The nutritionist suggested variations on the formula. We measured ingredients, counted calories, tested different brands and products, but nothing worked. The doctors told me to set the pump on drip and feed him all night so he'd get extra calories while he slept. But if he wriggled at all, the tube would pop out and the pump would be feeding the bed instead of Nathaniel. I half-slept, keeping guard.

I wanted to give him a life that seemed normal to me. Babies are supposed to have "tummy time" to strengthen their spines, but Nathaniel's g-tube made it very uncomfortable for him. I piled tons of blankets on the floor to cushion the tube and distracted him for as long as I could with books and pictures. His body was normal, and I didn't want the issues he had to cascade into new ones.

I had one mom friend at the time. Russel and I had met Denise and her husband at a parenting class at the Jewish Community Center in Hoboken while she and I were both pregnant. Her son Joshua was born two weeks before Nathaniel, and I was still pregnant when we went to his bris. It was only later that I learned Joshua was born without one of his hands. Ironically, Denise told me she had covered him up so I wouldn't see because she didn't want to make me nervous about my upcoming delivery. Then I had a baby with much more severe issues — Nathaniel couldn't even have a bris — so I could have used a little preparation. But we were still far from joking about that at the time.

On a good day, Denise and I could squeeze in a walk with the boys. The first time we went to the park, we tried to join a mommy group. They met with their strollers in a circle, presumably to talk about swaddling techniques and how their babies were sleeping and what diaper cream worked best. Denise and I tried to be a part of it, but our babies stood out, and the other new moms were kind of scared of us. Or maybe it was my envy that got in the way. In any case, our outings ended up being just the two of us.

Denise cried a lot. Although I did my share of crying, my exhaustion was the more dazzling feature of my social game. I was just so tired. I couldn't relax at night. Sometimes Denise would come over to our apartment, take one look at my face, and say, "You take a nap. I'll watch the boys; we'll put on Baby Einstein." I was great company.

Russel had returned to work, so except for our excursions with Denise and Joshua, Nathaniel and I were mostly at home alone, tethered to his g-tube. Though he could only hear muffled sounds, I wanted him to start listening to music because it was so important to me—before I married Russel, my whole life had revolved around playing the piano and studying music. It was part of what defined me, and I couldn't imagine my baby's life without it. I would turn on classical music, block my ears as best I could, then turn up the volume until I thought he'd be able to hear. I also sang and spoke loudly, close to his nonexistent ears. He was still too young to be responsive, but I hoped the sound was coming through.

*Nathaniel: When I look at baby pictures of myself, I just see a baby. Sure, there are some tubes and contraptions, but all babies seem to have a lot of gear. My experience looks like one thing on the outside, but I was just a kid, born the way I was. The face that I saw in the mirror made sense to me. Visits to doctors were routine. I grew up with the understanding that my face was more complicated than everyone else's—it didn't work as well—but that was my world. Some kid might have to deal with his helicopter mom, his twin brother, his asthma. I think you have to lose something to feel the loss. I was born this way, and my parents loved me just the same. They always told me that being different made me interesting. Maybe that's why it didn't occur to me to feel sorry for myself, or even to focus on the mirror. I have always just felt like myself.*

## 5. to breathe

Two weeks after we got home, in mid-March, we went to Long Island for a weekend to visit Russel's parents. They were renting an apartment while they built a retirement home in North Carolina. Russel's brothers lived nearby with their families, and this would be the first time their children—who hadn't been allowed in the NICU—were meeting Nathaniel. My mother-in-law made pot roast, her go-to family feast, and everyone took turns holding the baby.

He was already six weeks old, but otherwise it was almost a classic meet-the-newborn family weekend. Or it would have been except that over the course of a day—one day!—Nathaniel's breathing changed. He was sleeping next to me in a portable crib, and at one in the morning I woke up to hear him making a terrible snoring noise. Looking over, I saw that his chest was rising and falling too heavily. He was gasping for breath. I shook Russel awake.

"Something's not right."

We turned on the light. Nathaniel was turning blue. Russel called Dr. Bernstein, the ENT who had opened his nose. Dr. Bernstein was everything you want in a doctor: knowledgeable and gentle. And Russel had his home phone number. Of course he did. Wherever we went, Russel made friends. I've seen people treat nurses like servants, but Russel is always appreciative, and he always wants to know a little bit about everyone. He'll say, "Hey, what's your story? How is your life? Is there anything I can do for you? I'm going down to the cafeteria. Can I get you a cup of coffee?" Doctors, nurses, taxi drivers—Russel connects with everyone, and in Nathaniel's medicalized world, from the very beginning, it made everything more personal.

"This doesn't sound good," the doctor said. "You need to come to the hospital as soon as possible."

Dr. Bernstein surmised that his tongue had grown but his jaw hadn't, which was making it difficult for him to get enough air. He told us to keep him face down as we drove so his tongue would fall away from his throat.

It was at least an hour from my in-laws' house to the hospital. Russel drove, and I sat in the back with Nathaniel between my legs, his head facing the floor between my knees. So much for using a car seat; breathing takes priority over being buckled up for safety.

Russel drove as fast as he could on the icy roads, and we were lucky it was the middle of the night because at one point he lost control and we started spinning in circles in the middle of the highway. I was screaming. Russel was screaming. Dr. Bernstein, still on the phone, must have thought Long Island was going down in flames. When we skidded to a stop, there was a moment of silence, then we heard him say, "How's it going there, guys?"

An army of doctors met us in the ER. Nathaniel was given an emergency tracheotomy.

• • •

How was it that two weeks after bringing him home, there we were, back in the hospital with a baby who couldn't breathe? Why had they sent us home with a baby who could risk suffocating? I later found out that if Nathaniel had stayed in the hospital for thirty-one consecutive days after his birth, he would have qualified for Medicaid. That meant that whatever our insurance didn't cover would have been paid for. Hospitals try to avoid that, so we were sent home after 28 days, possibly too early, and every problem that followed was an insurance nightmare.

Dr. Bernstein had anticipated the natural growth of Nathaniel's tongue, but that was not the only complication. In his second surgery, when they had drilled a hole through the bone behind his nose, they placed a plastic stent in the hole to keep it open while he grew. To keep the airway clear, he needed to be suctioned through one of his nostrils whenever he started breathing heavily and through his mouth.

One day as I was nodding off in the chair next to Nathaniel's bassinet, I heard him crying and lifted my head to see my least-favorite nurse roughly shoving the suction into his nose. He let out a wail of pain. When she left I picked him up to comfort him and was horrified to see the stent hanging down in the back of his mouth. I called for a doctor, who examined Nathaniel. The nurse had pushed the suction in too recklessly; the stent poked through his palate.

The damage was done. The doctor explained that they would not be able to replace the stent for fear of further damaging his palate. They had removed it, hoping the airway would stay open on its own, but it was unlikely, and we knew that there was probably going to be a tracheotomy in his future. I'll always wonder what might have happened if we'd saved that working nose; would he have been able to avoid the tracheotomy?

After we left the hospital, the bone had grown more quickly than anyone expected, closing the medically created airway. We could have lost him that night.

The tracheotomy was not just a temporary emergency fix. The doctors inserted a tube that went from a hole in Nathaniel's neck (called the stoma) directly to his windpipe. Where the tube came out of the stoma there was a neck plate, which attached to a cotton neck strap called a trach tie that held the contraption in place. The g-tube he would outgrow someday, but the only way he would be able to get rid of the tracheostomy would be to have surgery to open the bone behind his nose. That bone, which had been soft and easy to open when he was a newborn, would harden and thicken and cause us no end of trouble.

When Nathaniel woke up from surgery his ability to make a sound was gone. The air that he exhaled was going out through the trach instead of through his voice box. Until he was big and strong enough to use a special valve for the trach, he would be silent. The only way I could tell when he was crying was that his mouth would be wide open, his face turning purple. A screaming baby with no voice. It was anguishing. My in-laws showed up at the hospital the next day. We all cried over Nathaniel, his tiny body now doubly medicalized. It was hard to swallow, no pun intended. With the g-tube and now the trach, he seemed even further from ever becoming a healthy, carefree kid. When I dreamed of "normal," I was dreaming of freedom from constantly fearing for his life.

This time, our discharge from the hospital involved confirmation that we knew how to keep the trach clean, suction it, and attach an ambu bag to it. (An ambu bag is a bag/mask that we used to force-feed air into Nathaniel's lungs in an emergency.)

When we left, I was able to cherish a brief moment of normalcy—the hospital staff clapping and taking pictures—but leaving came with the terrifying realization that there would be no doctor on duty. Our baby was back home, but we couldn't hear him cry. And if something went wrong, we were the ones who would have to figure it out. We were it.

The trach was a cruel savior. My new full-time job was keeping it clean and sterile. Everything that ordinarily runs down our throats, gets coughed up, or comes out our noses needed to be suctioned out of it. This involved attaching a skinny tube (a catheter) to a portable suction machine, then inserting the catheter down the trach into his lung. Sometimes I would hit the lung and see his silent, heartbreaking cry. I soon learned exactly how far to go. It was hard for him to breathe well while he was being suctioned, so I had to complete the task in five to ten seconds. When I pulled the catheter out, I held the neck plate in place so that the trach tube wouldn't come out with it. Day and night, I monitored his breath. When I heard it catch roughly, I suctioned him. Soon I could practically do it in my sleep (if you can call what I did sleeping): Roll over in bed. Check Nathaniel's breathing. Put on gloves. Suction. Sterilize the machine. Dispose of the catheter.

Here was a doozy: no water could get in the trach. None. Nathaniel loved his little blue bathtub that went on top of the sink, but he couldn't get wet from the neck up. He had cradle cap—I had to wash his head! I used a damp soft washcloth with a tiny bit of baby soap, but if water found its way around the trach tie and into his lungs, just like that, he could drown. I kept the suction machine next to the bathtub, grateful that at least it was battery operated and I didn't have to worry about electrocuting my baby on top of everything else.

The trach was pretty much an open wound so it was prone to infections. Or, rather, it invited infections and they flocked to it like ants to a sugar cube. The whole contraption had to be replaced frequently to limit the growth of bacteria, so every two weeks I took Nathaniel on the subway to the NYU Medical Center. Now, negotiating the subway steps with a stroller is a point of pride for New York moms, but I was too freaked out and nervous to applaud myself for adding the portable feeding pump, a suctioning pump, a bag full of formula, extra IV bags, sterile gloves, and one-use catheters in addition to a diaper bag. My "diaper bag" made me look like a medical supply salesperson.

To the hospital-room-chic décor we were cultivating at home, we added a huge, loud, vibrating oxygen machine with a humidifier that could be connected to Nathaniel's trach by a large hose. I also ordered shipments of gloves, vinegar for sterilizing, saline drops, peroxide, hundreds of catheters, an air compressor, a nebulizer bottle, aerosol tubing, a trach mask, sterile water, and saline ampules. It was a daunting amount of supplies that would go from overwhelming and incomprehensible to familiar in mere days. I entered monthly ordering reminders into my calendar: 2 trachs, 50 suction catheters, 30 t-vents.

Amid all this nursing and worry, there were tender moments. I watched Russel lie down on a couch with Nathaniel on his chest. They slept that way, a deep, peaceful sleep, for half an hour. For half an hour, life was normal. But for the most part during those first thirty days, or the first few months, or the first full year, it was difficult to completely enjoy the best moments because they were immediately preceded or followed by a complication, one more issue to overcome. When new parents ask Russel for advice, he always says, "Cherish every good moment because forty-five seconds later it's going to be gone, and the memory is all that will get you through." He's not talking about a first step, or saying "mama" for the first time. We didn't even have the wherewithal to anticipate those milestones. Russel means the moments when you can take a deep breath and savor the absence of worry.

Once, early on, Nathaniel got a trach infection. I had suctioned him forty times in one day and saw that soon I was going to run out of suction catheters. I couldn't suction him without a new catheter, and if I didn't suction him, he wouldn't be able to breathe. It was a weekend, which meant I couldn't call the supplier for overnight delivery, and we couldn't just walk into a drugstore to pick up more. In a panic, I called my new friend Jenna.

Jenna's daughter Emily, who was two years older than Nathaniel, also had Treacher Collins. I didn't know many families with kids who had the same syndrome as Nathaniel as most of the people I saw in the waiting room at NYU were there for cleft lips and palates. But even when I did see craniofacial families, I didn't socialize with them, mostly because I was too focused on Nathaniel, but also because some of them had a different attitude than I did. They would say, "We're so blessed. Thank you, God, for giving us this child."

I had a hard time with that. I would sit there thinking, *Are you serious? You don't have moments when you question God?* Their attitude seemed so fake to me. So it was great to find another mother in a similar situation who spoke my language.

When Nathaniel first got his trach, I was still having a hard time coming to terms with the life my baby had ahead of him. I was ridiculously focused on his face more than on the medical issues. How would he lead a happy life being so deformed? How would he find his way socially? When I called Jenna, her calm, sweet voice comforted me.

She began telling me about her daughter. "Emily goes to preschool. Her body and mind are fine. She does this, she does that." She reassured me that Nathaniel would have friends, he'd go to school, he'd be able to swing at the playground. As she spoke, I began crying with relief and joy. It would be okay. He'd have a normal life.

Jenna and I clicked, and from then on if I wanted to cry to someone, I called her.

When we ran out of catheters that Saturday night, I called Jenna and asked if she had catheters left over from when Emily had a trach. She did, so even though it was the middle of the night, Russel drove over to her Brooklyn townhouse—about an hour away —to pick them up.

When he got home two hours later, he dropped the box of catheters on the kitchen counter and crashed. He only had a couple hours to sleep before he left for Long Island. His brother was finishing his basement, and Russel had promised to help with the drywall. I stayed home with Nathaniel.

The catheters were in the same factory box that mine came in, still sealed. Later that morning, when I needed one, I used a knife to slice through the sealing tape. The moment I pulled up the first flap, hundreds of cockroaches flew out at me. My hand was instantly black with them. It was like a horror movie. I freaked out, flinging the roaches off my hands. I grabbed Nathaniel, the bag with the pump in it, and my phone, and escaped from the apartment. I called Russel from the hallway.

"They're everywhere!" I screamed. "Help!" Russel thought I

was being murdered. It took a solid minute of screaming before I managed to communicate to him that I was living my nightmare.

"Okay, Magda, go back in. Get your wallet and keys. Make sure you have everything, then leave the apartment."

Following his instructions, I went back in and discovered the roaches had formed a long line, hundreds of them marching down the kitchen counter and across the floor. I grabbed my stuff and closed the door behind me. If they wanted the apartment, they could have it.

Back out in the hallway, I did my best to clean a used catheter and suctioned Nathaniel. I was supposed to use a new catheter every time, but I decided that a dirty catheter was better than roaches.

Russel ditched the renovation and came home to help me. We called an exterminator and scheduled him to bomb the apartment.

Meanwhile, we packed up our bags and supplies and went to Russel's parents' house on Long Island. En route, we called Nurse Pat at NYU. Nurse Pat Chibbaro was one of our favorite nurses and she'd become a friend. We begged her for enough catheters to get us through the weekend, then drove to the hospital to pick them up. It wouldn't be the last time we turned to our medical family at NYU for emergency supplies.

# 6. a different world

The world is not always kind to a woman with a special needs baby.

I went to NYU often, sometimes three times a week, to make sure Nathaniel's equipment was in good order and to check for infections. From Hoboken, I would take a twenty-minute commuter train to Penn Station, then walk crosstown from the west side of Manhattan to the east — about a mile.

One time I took him to an appointment during an absolutely miserable snowstorm. It was bitterly cold, and I was already feeling sorry for myself because nobody had offered to help me carry the stroller up from the subway. It had equipment hanging from both sides, and as I struggled to haul it up the stairs, a grey stream of Wall Street commuters pushed past. Exiting Penn Station, I saw that the sidewalks hadn't been shoveled and I knew it would be impossible to maneuver the stroller. I would have to take a cab.

The cab line was very long. Nathaniel was bundled up, but I was worried about him, and I was so cold myself. I looked around plaintively, but everyone pretended not to see me. Not a soul offered to let me go ahead. I went to the front of the line and said, "I have a baby. It's so cold. Can I please take one of the next cabs?"

They all shook their heads: No, sorry. We're in a rush.

It became clear that nobody was going to help me. I was utterly alone.

I called Russel. "What am I supposed to do?" I choked through sobs. "Nobody is helping me."

"Go to the front of the line," he said. "Don't even ask. Just get in the next cab."

He was so clear and certain in that moment, but later he would tell me that he was at a loss. What was the right thing to do? Should he ditch the meeting he was in and run across town to help me?

From the outside, it looked like we divided responsibilities along "traditional" gender lines: I was the daily caregiver, the primary parent to feed and nurture Nathaniel. I handled supplies and fought the daily battle against bacteria to avoid infections.

Russel was the provider. He also kept track of the details of Nathaniel's medical record, paid the bills, argued with insurers. And he was always the first to learn all the medical procedures. Russel worked; I stayed home to care for the children, cook, and clean.

But Russel often struggled with his role. Should he come home and help me when I was at my wits' end, or should he give everything to the career that would provide for his family? Early on, every time we went to the hospital, we were surrounded by families who were completely reliant on Medicaid, Medicare, food stamps. Russel didn't want that life. He knew that it would take a lot of money to care for our family, more than he was making, so he decided that from eight to five every day his responsibility to us was to excel in his career. That's why he didn't come to Penn Station to help me, and he often couldn't be there with me when Nathaniel was sick. Though he went to every single surgery, there were infinite in-betweens when he couldn't be with us. We survived, but Russel always felt like he was letting us down. And yes, I wanted him there—he was the only person I trusted with Nathaniel—but it was impossible.

Calling Russel on the phone was my best lifeline, but I didn't have the moxie to take his advice and cut the taxi line. I couldn't believe that no one would help a mother with a baby, especially in that weather, but I didn't want to make a scene. And so I walked. By the time I got to the hospital my cheeks were red, my feet were wet, my fingers frozen. I went into a room with Nurse Pat and cried. "People are so mean. I don't know how I'm going to do it."

That first year I was kicking hard to keep my head above water, and when I paused, often it was only to see how far away I still was from dry land. On another snowy day, after one of Nathaniel's appointments in the city, I was walking home from the train station in Hoboken. I knew Nathaniel and I were both starting to get colds, so I stopped at a local pediatrician that was near our apartment. For all the specialists we had access to in the city, for something as mundane as a cold, this office, with its two nice Polish doctors, was the easiest resource.

The waiting room was full of moms, each with a seemingly perfect baby and a textbook reason for being there: a checkup, a spot of eczema, a cough. I took Nathaniel out of his stroller and put him on my lap. His thin, sweet arms; his face swollen from his most recent surgery. In unison, the other mothers averted their eyes, pity and relief on their faces. This life, the winter, the medical equipment surrounding me, all of these people with these perfect babies. I sank into self-pity, down, under water. The doctors guided me to a private room where I wailed in Polish, "It's just so bad. Why did this happen to me?" They offered me the only comfort that there was: He was alive, he needed me, it was hard, I would have to be strong—the only comfort there was to offer. It was nothing revelatory, but hearing those words in my native tongue helped carry them to my soul.

How often, settled on the subway, would this happen: I would catch the eye of another mother, her baby neatly tucked in a stroller or a sling, a stylish diaper bag slung comfortably over her shoulder. We might exchange a smile, and for a minute I would taste what it might be like to be part of an unspoken community of new moms. But as soon as she caught a glimpse of Nathaniel, she would look away, trying not to stare. There it was, an instinct to be polite but also to shield herself from the horrible reality, the possibility that such things happen, that my life could have been hers. We lived in different worlds. I tried to steer myself away from the useless jealous thought that her life could have been mine, but during that first year, I often walked down the street pushing Nathaniel's stroller and crying.

Some days were brighter, and Nathaniel and I would navigate our little world as if we'd chosen this adventure. We walked through Hoboken together, its tree-lined streets strung with cafes and shops. In the early evening, I would push the stroller through town to meet Russel's train. It was a fifteen-minute walk, and as the stores I passed became familiar, I started to exchange hellos with the people who worked there. With the hood of the stroller down to protect Nathaniel from wind and sun, his face wasn't exposed. I looked and felt like every other mom.

On the walk home from the train station the three of us would stop at the market for a piece of fresh fish or meat, and when we got home Russel and I would cook together, with music on the stereo and Nathaniel watching from his little chair. He was an easy baby that way, bless him, always content to watch and entertain himself, never fussing. Sometimes it seemed like he was grateful for every moment the doctors weren't messing with his body.

Often, at 3:00 a.m., we would bundle him up, put him in the stroller, and walk the narrow streets of Hoboken. It was a couple of blocks through our neighborhood to the main street. On one of our first moonlight walks, we saw steam coming out the back door to a bakery. The light was on, a gold beacon in the still-dark morning.

A couple of young guys were carrying boxes from the basement into the bakery. They noticed us, waved, and one said, "What are you doing out here with a stroller in the middle of the night?"

We told them our baby couldn't sleep. Indeed, Nathaniel was

wide awake, happily taking it all in. They were friendly guys, and they insisted on giving us fresh-baked rolls. I tried to pay for them, but they wouldn't let me.

Our hands were cold, and the rolls were straight out of the oven, almost too hot to hold. They smelled so good, the warm, comforting smell of home, we had to eat them on the spot. After that the bakery workers looked for us every night.

"Why weren't you here yesterday?" they would ask if they hadn't seen us.

"Oh, yesterday was a good night," we'd tell them. Here and there, there were nights when we had a home-cooked meal, a glass of wine, an evening walk, and Nathaniel would sleep peacefully through the night without needing to be suctioned, but in winter those evenings were rare. No new parents love being awake in the middle of the night with a restless baby, but those rolls were so tasty they almost made it worth it.

# 7. not cut out for this

As hard as Russel was working—he got two promotions during the first two years of Nathaniel's life—money was immediately a problem. Most of the doctors at NYU didn't take insurance. The bills poured in, many for each surgery: the anesthesiologist, the surgeons, the hospital stay, and so on. The total for a surgery might be anywhere from $5,000 to $60,000 if Nathaniel had three procedures in one fell swoop. Russel was constantly on the phone with insurance companies, negotiating for higher reimbursements. Fighting with the insurance companies was a full-time job. We wouldn't have been able to afford the amount they didn't cover, but an organization called the National Foundation for Facial Reconstruction (or NFFR, now called myFace) often paid the rest.

Somehow there were always more bills. $15,000 here. $10,000 there. The bills would come and we were expected to pay them out of pocket. Our credit took a hit as we waited for reimbursements from insurance and the NFFR to kick in. One day I was at the grocery store with a cart full of food, and when I went to pay, my debit card was denied. Our bank account was frozen.

I had to go home from the grocery store with no food. *There's always a soup to be made*, I thought. When I was little, food was in short supply under the Communist government in Poland. My grandma often made a meal out of rice baked with apples, cinnamon, and sugar. That night, I cooked what I found in our apartment: It was rice and apples for dinner. We had to find ways to get by until Russel straightened out the credit card situation, but I knew if my grandmother could make it work, so would I.

The $1,500 rent in Hoboken was too much. We would have to move.

Russel's brother Hal and his wife, Nancy, offered to build an apartment in their basement for us — this was the apartment that Russel had been helping to finish when I was attacked by killer cockroaches.

Hal and Nancy lived in Wading River, on the north fork of Long Island, in a two-story house. They'd generously finished the basement, dividing it into a living room, bedroom, kitchenette, and bathroom. Hal added wall-to-wall carpeting and finished the walls, doing his best to make it welcoming for us. We moved there when Nathaniel was around six months old.

Now Russel commuted two and a half hours each way to work: driving for an hour, then catching a train, then hopping on the subway. I stayed in the basement, slowly feeding Nathaniel for hours at a time, trying to keep the environment sterile. When Russel, Hal, and Nancy got home, I had dinner waiting for them. I love to cook, and it was the only way I could think of to try to thank them for putting us up. But if Nathaniel was sick, I couldn't take my attention off him long enough to prepare a meal. Then I stayed down in the basement, keeping vigil to make sure he didn't choke.

The first time Nathaniel's trach fell out was in Hal and Nancy's basement. He was about six months old, and I was accustomed to waking up every thirty minutes to check on him. His crib was right beside the bed. I'd reach over to feel the g-tube and the trach, sometimes without even opening my eyes. But on this night I woke up at 2:00 in the morning and his breathing sounded different. When I reached over, I felt the trach tube. It was supposed to be inside his neck, but it had been dislodged, and I didn't know how long it had been that way. The doctors had told us that if this happened, we would only have fifteen minutes to get it back in place before the tissue would start to tighten and it would need to be surgically replaced. More critically, we didn't know how long Nathaniel could survive breathing through his mouth.

We'd been taught how to replace the tube, but neither of us had ever actually done it. Cradling Nathaniel, Russel walked up the basement stairs, opened the door, and stepped into the living room. He looked up to the second floor and saw his brother Hal, the big brother he had looked up to his whole life, standing at the top of the stairs in his underwear, with bedhead. Hal took in the scene and said, "I just can't do this. I can't help." Then he turned and went back into his bedroom.

Russel put Nathaniel on the kitchen table. It was a long,

wooden farmer's table, and above it was an overhead light by which Russel could see. The trach tube had to go into the hole in Nathaniel's neck (the stoma) at just the right angle.

Russel tried to wiggle it back into place, but the hole started bleeding. I hovered over my baby, fretting uselessly. Russel tried again and again. Nathaniel was getting agitated, and I started to freak out. Pacing, fretting, praying, I was a basket case.

Ungodly noises were coming from Nathaniel, a sound Russel now describes as a death gurgle, but at the time he said, "The bubbling means he's breathing." He was trying to reassure us both that our son wasn't about to die.

I'm squeamish, and in a normal world putting a Band-Aid on a skinned knee would have been a challenge for me. I'd been making good progress with the daily care that Nathaniel required, but in a situation like this, I was utterly useless. Russel had been a lifeguard and a camp counselor, and knew CPR, though he'd never had to use it. This didn't mean he was medically prepared for the prolonged emergency of caring for Nathaniel, not remotely — but temperamentally, he had what it took. He rose to the responsibility, calm and confident in the middle of a crisis.

He ordered me to call 911. Shaking in panic, I dialed the number. They said, "What is the address of the emergency?"

"911!" I screamed. "911!" Telling the operator the number I had just dialed instead of our address was not exactly helpful. This may be hard to believe, but I had never been a nervous person — I'd never had anything to be nervous about. That changed forever the day Nathaniel was born. Now that I couldn't control what was happening, I was always nervous, and in emergencies I panicked and couldn't think straight.

Russel grabbed the phone from me and gave the operator Hal's address. Finally, the ambulance arrived and took us to a local hospital. I was worried because it wasn't his regular hospital, and the stoma looked scary because it was still bleeding from Russel's failed attempts. It didn't take them long to put the trach back in, but I didn't relax until they showed me that his oxygen level was good and I saw that he was comfortable. He fell asleep almost right away, and then I was fine. But I worried that it would happen again and was on high alert for a week or two after that.

Later I would look back at this as the moment I knew what role Russel would play in our family. I could handle the day-to-day, but in an emergency, I fell apart. Russel was very emotional—he'd often cry after a rough medical moment—but in an emergency he took charge. No matter how bad it got, no matter how tense and gross, Russel knew exactly how to manage the situation and how to keep Nathaniel safe until we got to a medical professional.

I met Russel when I was twenty-two years old. It was my fourth trip to America—I'd been coming for vacations, sponsored by an aunt, ever since I was nineteen. The summer we met, I'd just finished my third year of college in Poland. My cousin, who'd grown up in New York, got me a job as a nanny in the Hamptons.

My employers, Rich and Vanessa, were part of a wealthy summer circle. Maybe not the cream of the Hamptons crop—instead of mansions with private beaches they stayed in a hotel called Dune Deck that opened directly onto the ocean. My employer and her friends spent their days sitting in the sun by the pool, wearing Prada and Gucci, smoking and starving themselves. Some of these mothers brought babysitters with them and some didn't, but all of them seemed to spend their time drinking wine at 10:30 in the morning, going shopping, or working out with their personal trainers. I watched my employer buy designer bags, then hide them under the bed so her husband wouldn't know how much she'd spent. Now I recognize that behavior as a stereotype of the upper-class housewife, but then even that small gesture of indulgence and deceit was completely foreign to me.

These husbands and wives lived separate lives. Rich spent the week working in Manhattan and then arrived in the Hamptons on Thursday afternoon, played golf all day Friday and Saturday, and left on Sunday. He would go out with Vanessa at night, but didn't find much time for their son, Hunter. The fourth summer I worked for them, the marriage appeared to be on the verge of collapse.

I wasn't in the Hamptons to party and I took my job seriously. I wanted Hunter to have friends, so I'd invite the other kids to our room, make them a snack, then take them all to play ball. Some moms noticed and happily handed them over to me; others had no idea where their children were and didn't seem to care. The dads were already off playing golf.

After three summers of this, my idea of America was this strange, privileged life, with its forgotten children. It made no sense to me. Then along came Russel.

Vanessa was the one who pointed him out to me. Except on weekends, my work finished around 7:00 p.m., so I had my evenings to myself. One night, Vanessa asked me my plans, and I told her I was going to read in my room.

She said, "We've got to find you a boyfriend!"

I'd never had a boyfriend before, not even close. I was raised as a strict Polish Catholic, and I didn't have any plans to date. I thought that one day I would find a husband—I had no idea how—and that would be it. When some of the men who worked at the hotel would come by my room to ask me out, I was scared. My English wasn't great. They didn't know me. And some were twice my age! I figured the only reason they were knocking was because they were interested in sex, so I wouldn't even open the door. When Vanessa explained that being asked out on dates was normal, even desirable, I still resisted. She wasn't exactly my role model. Besides, I wasn't planning on staying in America, so why would I want to get involved with someone just to leave in a few months? I was going to return to school, finish my studies, and become a music professor.

Vanessa kept pushing me to date. One day, while we were watching Hunter play basketball, she said, "There's a nice Jewish boy who works here. He's handsome and he went to law school. I think he likes you; you should give him a chance." You could see everyone coming and going from where we were sitting, so when Russel happened to walk by, she pointed him out to me.

In spite of my disinterest, I started noticing him more and more. Russel stood out because he'd stop to pay attention to the kids whenever he walked past. He'd start up a game of tag with them or tussle with Vanessa's dog. No one else did this—neither the men who tried to date me nor the children's own parents.

My parents had always told me that children and animals can tell if a person is good. You can trust their instincts, so I knew that this guy who stopped to play with the kids had to be a good person.

There were some machinations going on behind the scenes. One night, one of the waitresses, Eileen, invited me to come with her to a bar up the road. Russel ordinarily worked at the restaurant at Dune Deck, but "coincidentally" he was bartending there that night.

Before then, we'd only had a few conversations over the heads of the children as he was on his way to work, while I was focused on making sure everyone was safe and having fun. Now, for the first time, we were both relaxed, sitting at the bar and talking with no distractions. This was easy for me, but it meant that Russel was a horrible bartender. At one point he even asked a friend of his to make his own drink—I would later find out it was because he didn't want to interrupt our conversation.

I thought he was handsome. He was tall with dark hair, and he was always smiling. But what was most important was that the more we spoke, the more he confirmed my parents' theory of dog and child character judgment. Of all the men who had asked me out, Russel was the only one who actually tried to get to know me. He asked me questions about myself, and I learned that, having completed law school, he had decided he didn't want to be a lawyer. He was thirty-three years old and, by his own report, having an early midlife crisis. Recently divorced, he was sleeping on a friend's couch while bartending and managing a golf course to pay back his student loans. If you ask him, he'll say he was a loser.

The friend who owned the couch, Steven Dietz, told Russel, "This has to stop. This can't be your life. You're a good dude, I love you, but you gotta get a job." Then Steven drove him to a bar in Westhampton named Starr Boggs after its celebrity chef. He went up to the manager and said, "This is my buddy, Russel. If you don't give him a job I'm going to kill him." That was how he'd started working at the tiki bar overlooking the dunes and serving vodka martinis to New York City housewives after their morning workouts.

At some point I asked him, "Where is your passion?"

He blushed and said, "Isn't it a little too soon for me to express my passion?"

I tried again. "What are your interests? Is there something wrong with that question?"

He says he thought my broken English was adorable.

At the end of the night, he asked me to teach him some Polish words. I taught him how to say, "Hello, my name is Russel.

It's a pleasure to meet you," and wrote out the pronunciation on the back of a taxicab business card. He still has it in a drawer, either for sentimental reasons or because his Polish hasn't improved much in the last fifteen years. He was a very quick learner, but life got in the way.

After that night, I may have watched from the deck to see when his car pulled into the parking lot, but I'll never admit it. He started asking me to go out with him, but I was old-fashioned and didn't really think of myself as a person who did that. If I dated, it would be because I thought I'd met my husband, and now was not the time or place. I had school to finish.

But Russel is a force of nature and he finally won me over. I agreed to a proper date, and after that we slowly got to know each other better. Before I met Russel, I would visit my cousin in Manhattan on the weekends, but during the week I was very alone, so I was happy to have found someone who genuinely cared about me. Now I'd meet him when he showed up for work, and we'd talk and he'd play with Hunter before it was time for him to bartend or wait tables. As the summer went on, I began staying up late, waiting eagerly to see him. When his shift ended after midnight, he'd sneak over to my room, though I had strict rules for us. I was still very chaste, and I knew how gossipy the hotel staff was, so I didn't want anyone to see him coming into my room.

I only had a small refrigerator, so while I couldn't really cook for him, I always made him a snack. And he always ate it, whether he was hungry or not. We talked about our days, gossiped about the summer people, and just connected quickly and easily. Our romance lasted the whole summer, deepening as the weeks passed.

I was supposed to fly back to Poland on September 12, 2001. I'd spent a few days at my cousin's apartment in Manhattan before returning home, and planned to head to my aunt's in Westhampton for the last night before I departed. On the morning of 9/11, I was walking across town to Penn Station when I saw fire and smoke coming out of one of the Twin Towers. Something was happening, but I had no idea what. I headed underground into Penn Station, where I got caught up in a big crowd looking at train schedules and standing in line for tickets. At first it wasn't clear that the trains were canceled, but more and more people gathered, and the lines didn't move at all. Finally there was an announcement to evacuate. I don't know how much time had passed, but when I'd walked into the station, it had been a sunny morning, and when I came out, the sky was overcast, dust was falling, and the Twin Towers had disappeared. People were running in all directions, and everything was closed. I didn't have a cell phone, so I found a payphone and left a message for Russel. Then I got through to my mother in Poland, who told me that she was watching the news and they were saying it was a terrorist attack.

The tragedy of 9/11 brought Russel and me closer. My flight was delayed for almost a week, so he invited me to stay with him at his brother Hal's house on Long Island, where he was living. I wasn't entirely comfortable with the scenario, but I knew I needed to be with him. I said goodbye to my aunt and took my things to Long Island. In the days that followed, as the city mourned, we spent quiet time together, going to the beach or for a long drive. I met more of Russel's family, and he made it clear that he was serious about us staying together. By the time I left for Poland, Russel had already bought a plane ticket to come visit me.

I went back to my fourth year of music school and settled into my routine. There was no Skype back then, so Russel called me every day, burning through international phone cards. After he finished his shift waiting tables, he would sit in his car in the driveway so as not to disturb Hal and his wife, Nancy, and wait until 1:00 a.m. so he could call when I was waking up in Poland. The switchboard phone at my music school dormitory was always answered by the house mother, and I taught Russel how to say, *Dzien dobry Pani Haniu. Magda prosze?* which meant, "Hello Mrs. Hania. Magda please?"

Then the house mother would open the door of her office and shout, "Magda, telefon!" and patch him through to my room.

When I came to the phone Russel would say, "I just want to be the first voice you hear when you wake up in the morning." It was nice to be told I was missed and to be given a positive boost for the day. I felt special. I was learning to be in love, and to be loved.

After the horror show with the trach in Hal's basement, the possibility of it getting dislodged constantly loomed over us. Nathaniel was getting old enough to start learning how to keep himself safe. Whenever he started to fiddle with his trach or his g-tube — we called them his buttons — I'd say, "No, don't touch. It's not a toy." It was like what most parents teach a baby about a hot stove, except imagine that there are three burners on and the stove is within the baby's reach at all times.

Nathaniel quickly learned to be careful, but he developed an allergy to a plastic part of the trach. It would get itchy, and sometimes he would pull it out when he scratched. Russel, who would have been an excellent doctor or nurse because he wasn't the least bit squeamish, got the hang of changing it. But I always panicked and gagged, and though I could do it in an emergency, for a long time, I'd take Nathaniel to the doctor to do it if Russel wasn't available. After about two years, I got so tired of the drive and the inconvenience, and I had seen it done so many times, that I learned to just suck it up and do it myself without freaking out.

• • •

Along with the normal developmental milestones — crawling, talking, doing puzzles, etc. — we had bigger ones we were trying to reach. Mile*boulders*. The first was feeding Nathaniel through his mouth.

Not long after we moved to Long Island, when Nathaniel was six months old, he had his first mandibular distraction, a surgery to try to expand his jaw and give him more room to eat. Each jaw distraction actually involved several surgeries: the first to put in the expansion device, the second to lock the expanded jaw in place, and the third to remove the device. His craniofacial surgeon, Dr. Joseph McCarthy, had, with colleagues, pioneered this surgery to help kids like Nathaniel. Dr. McCarthy was kind of a god in our new world.

Nathaniel would have around five more jaw distractions in the first eleven years of his life.

Nathaniel came home from the surgery with pins in his jaw that had to be turned every day in order to gently stretch the bone and allow new bone to fill the space. *Pins. Gently. Stretch.* These are the words the doctors used, and later it struck me how falsely yogic they are. Just a little baby acupuncture on a Sunday afternoon. A mother-baby yoga class. Yeah, not so much. This miracle of modern medicine looked and felt more like medieval torture.

Russel was the obvious choice to do the pin-turning, but often he was traveling and it fell to me. I would start the process by crying and throwing up (the first sign this wasn't exactly a baby spa). Then, terrified that I would slip and hurt my baby, I would lie him down and kneel over him, my knees on his hands to prevent him from moving. (Forceful restraint: also not covered in mother-baby yoga manuals.) I would count to ten, then put the screwdriver in with one hand and hold his head with the other. I turned the screwdriver and could feel his jawbone stretching. Then blood would start dribbling down either side of his head. (Mother-baby yoga class officially up in flames.) I'd throw up again, then everything would be fine until the next day when I'd have to repeat this torture.

> *Nathaniel: When you think about it, it's pretty crazy to be tortured by your own loving mother when you're an infant. The same person who cuddles you 99 percent of the time then takes a screwdriver, sits on top of you, and hurts you. My mom says I cried in pain every time. I don't remember any of it, but I have to think that because my parents did it with love, not out of anger or rage, I wasn't psychologically damaged. My grandmother says that babies feel energy. So maybe these experiences scarred me. But maybe they made me strong. Maybe both. All I can report is that I'm okay so far.*

## 8. to eat, to speak

Just because his jaw was now slightly bigger didn't mean that Nathaniel automatically understood how to eat. I'd put baby food on a spoon and he'd hold it in his mouth, but he didn't know that the idea was to swallow it. He'd never had to wrap his young head around the concept of swallowing. You'd think it would be instinctive, like nursing. Maybe it was, but when nursing went out the window, so did swallowing. If I pushed food down his throat, he'd choke. His brain just didn't have a relationship with how to eat.

A speech and occupational therapist from the special needs and children's services organization on Long Island started coming to the basement twice a week. I can't remember her name, but I looked forward to her visits. It was the only chance I had to chat with someone close to my age, and I asked her all about her life. Nathaniel liked the therapy. She had different techniques to stimulate saliva production so he'd be motivated to swallow — she'd massage his cheek muscles or give him a pacifier with a hole in it, and she had a special spoon, like a big plastic Q-tip, that she'd put peanut butter or Cool Whip on for him to eat, and to this day peanut butter is one of his favorite foods.

These little tastes that she fed him didn't make a dent in his caloric needs for the day, so we were still dependent on giving him formula through the g-tube, which he was still throwing up so violently that he gave himself a stomach hernia. To help his reflux, Nathaniel had had a surgery called a fundoplication, where the doctor wraps the top of the stomach around the lower esophagus to make it harder for food to come up the wrong way. It helped for a while, but over time it had loosened. Now the doctors scheduled a second surgery to tighten it. They would also repair the hernia. Russel wanted to know when they were going to put the "fun" in "fundoplication." Between jaw surgeries and something with his tongue and attempts to open his nose, we had lost count of how many surgeries he had at this point. It was around eight. They were handing them out to us like presents at Christmas.

This medicalized, failed baby-feeding was completely antithetical to the way I grew up. My family had an organic farm in Sanok, a village in the Carpathian Mountains near the Ukraine border. My five siblings and I ate whatever my mother gave us. There was no such thing as pickiness. We ate or we went hungry.

My father grew potatoes, tomatoes, corn, fruits, and other vegetables on his farm, but for some reason Russia, which had controlled Poland since World War II, also controlled the meat in our lives. There wasn't a meat shortage — it was a question of ownership. If you wanted to keep your own pig, you had to hide it illegally. My mother kept a few chickens tucked away so we could have eggs. Everything at the supermarket except for bread, vodka, and cigarettes was rationed. That's right—protein was restricted, but you could drink and smoke with wild abandon. I guess they figured the best way to govern was to keep everyone in a constant state of oblivion.

Every week a family could get, say, two pounds of red meat, two pounds of kielbasa, two pounds of pork, and one pound of chicken. This meat did not sit in the butcher's refrigerator, available for purchase. Instead, the store would receive a limited amount twice a week. If you got to the store at 5:00 a.m. to wait on line, you might get a better quality of kielbasa, or there would still be some chicken left. But if you didn't get there until 8:00, you might wait in line for three hours only to score a very fatty piece of meat, barely good enough for broth, or you'd go home empty-handed. The same was true for sugar. And toilet paper.

Sometimes, if a neighbor slaughtered a contraband pig, my father would secretly trade vegetables and potatoes for a chunk of it. They'd bring it over in the dark of night, after curfew, wearing dark clothes, and cut it up in the basement by flashlight. Ordinary people were driven to extremes to put a little meat on the table. But no matter how hard-won our food was, meals were always loud, full of chatter, laughter, and the clinking of cutlery, with me, my two siblings who were closest in age, and often cousins at the table. This is what family was to me, an imperceptible bond that was built and reinforced every day at that boisterous table. I wanted to replicate it in my new home.

When Nathaniel was seven months old, my mother said, "Babies at this age should start eating solid foods like apples and bananas." I had always believed in real, whole foods like the ones we grew on our farm. Formula supposedly contained all the nutrients he needed, but not if he kept throwing it all up — so I went rogue and tried sending some tasty real food up through the g-tube.

First, I blended a little banana with water and put it into the tube, and, miraculously, he kept it down. The next day, in the grocery store, I noticed other mothers pondering the long shelves full of jars of organic baby food. It looked so much more appealing than chemical formula, so I picked one up. Why shouldn't I try it? His stomach was like everyone else's (except for the hernia). I put a few jars in my cart, and that night I emptied some sweet potato mush into the Vitamix, watered it down, and blended it until it was thin. Then I shoved it through the g-tube with syringes. Again, he kept it down. I couldn't have been happier to know that I was finally nourishing my baby with good, healthy food.

Growing up, my mother had fed us soup almost all winter using the fruits and vegetables she'd pickled and canned the rest of the year. One room in our basement had a damp, flat mud floor where she kept root vegetables in the winter — piles of potatoes, carrots, and parsley root. Another room had shelves and a high window where we stored jars of pickles, tomatoes, mushrooms, compote, jams, and jellies.

I soon realized I could water down whatever I made for dinner in the blender for Nathaniel. His doctor agreed that I could try this. There was a bit of trial and error — a few times we had to make a quick run to the doctor because I'd clogged the g-tube. And I still needed to track his intake and feed him for hours a day because the watered-down food filled him up before he'd eaten enough calories. But for the first time in his life, he had actual food in his belly. He sensed the food as I loaded it in, and as the warm soup settled in his stomach, I pretended to myself that he could somewhat taste it. At the very least, he had to be burping up good flavors for the first time in his life.

My mom says if you know how to make soup, you'll always have a meal because soup can be made from whatever is around. The base is always the same: onions, garlic, chicken stock, and whatever vegetables you have. That is my mother's homespun wisdom in a nutshell. *There's always a soup to be made* is her way of telling me to make the best of every situation.

Soon I was putting Nathaniel in his high chair to play with mashed bananas and potatoes and be part of the family during dinner. He still wasn't really eating, but at least his high chair was finally as messy and used as any baby's. I counted all the calories he took in through baby food and his g-tube and made sure he was getting enough protein, fruit, and vegetables. It was a lot of work, but I refused to believe he'd go through life with a tube in his stomach, and I did everything I could to help him reach that goal. My whole life was devoted to helping Nathaniel grow and develop.

At last, he started gaining weight. He was still so thin, but he was thriving.

The day came when he was scheduled to have the fundoplication. Nathaniel was eight months old and had been nibbling real food and receiving it through his g-tube for about six weeks. The hospital staff prepped Nathaniel, took his vitals, and set up an IV. He was in his little green gown and socks, and Russel was in his scrubs.

As we walked toward the operating room, the doctor turned to me and asked, "What's new?" Dr. Ginsburg, who had put in Nathaniel's g-tube, was the chief of pediatric surgery at NYU. He was a tall, handsome guy who carried himself with great confidence and had a reputation for odd bedside manners. The nurses told us he never opened up to patients, but we found him to be very friendly. When our paths crossed in the hospital, he always stopped to ask how we were doing.

Now I told the doctor that Nathaniel had started eating real food and was keeping it down.

"That's good news! When did he last throw up?" he asked.

"About a month ago," I replied.

We were in the middle of the hallway leading to the OR. Dr. Ginsburg stopped in his tracks. There was nearly a comical pileup as the rest of us halted behind him. He said, "He's keeping everything down! What are you doing here? Go home!" He instructed the nurses to remove the IV and told us to dress Nathaniel and take him home. "I'm not going to mess with him," he said. "The hernia will most likely heal itself." And it did. This was a huge payoff for finally finding the confidence to follow my instincts. I had been on completely foreign ground, but I was starting to find my footing.

From the moment he got the trach, Nathaniel could only make raspy, croaky noises. He couldn't scream. Most new moms want nothing more than for their babies to stop crying. But when his little face turned red, I yearned to hear my baby express his hunger or distress.

Around the same time as the canceled fundoplication, we found out that Nathaniel was ready for a Passy Muir. This was something we had been waiting for. The Passy Muir is a one-way valve that goes on the trach and is designed to help people speak. It let Nathaniel breathe in air, but it didn't let the air back out, forcing him to open his mouth to exhale. That meant air would get to his vocal cords, allowing him to talk.

Dr. Bernstein, the ENT surgeon, said that his lung capacity

had grown and he was physically bigger. It was time to give the Passy Muir a try. As they attached it to his trach, the doctors warned us that eight-month-old Nathaniel might freak out when he heard his own sounds for the first time. We stood waiting, pump at the ready in case he choked. But as soon as they put it in, a small, raspy sound came through his throat. He was comically surprised, looking left and right as if to say, "Who was that?" Then he started babbling and smiling.

I said, "You have such a cute voice!"

And from then on he never shut up.

Talking, tasting—Nathaniel grabbed on to each new sense that came his way and never let go. As his first autumn passed, he started wanting food. He'd sit in his high chair and wave his arms, bouncing and babbling in hope of applesauce or bananas. For a long time, every time I fed him through his g-tube or his mouth I was nervous that he would throw up. I was so used to that. The minute I ditched the formula though, he never threw up again and we had one less specialist on our regular appointment list.

I wanted all of the medical elements of our situation to be temporary. Normal is a door to a lot of different rooms, and normal was my goal. I wanted Nathaniel to be able to do all the things that most babies and kids did. I knew he might need a g-tube for future surgeries and another family like ours might keep it and continue feeding him that way in anticipation of that, but I wanted him to learn to eat by mouth because it brought him, and our family, one step closer to a regular life.

Nathaniel's ability to eat solids didn't happen overnight; it took a few good months of feeding him one spoonful at a time. His windpipe and his throat were so close together that he often choked. If food went down into the trach, I had to suction it. If he swallowed wrong, food came out through the stoma. The trach pump had to be within reach at all times. *I* had to be within reach at all times. Walking on a balance beam is easy and safe when you're two inches off the ground, but terrifying and dangerous when you're fifty feet in the air. Feeding a baby with a trach was like walking the high beam. The pump and I were the safety net.

My child's ability to breathe was always at risk. Every day had life-threatening possibilities, and every day my chest hurt—a weird, pinching pain that was now a constant. My brain had been rewired to be on alert all the time, and the clutch of worry was unrelenting.

## 9. to hear

The first thing I had noticed when Nathaniel was born was that he was missing ears. Growing up, my hearing was everything to me.

Right next to my parents' farm was a house that has since been torn down. It was an old-fashioned little wooden house, painted black. My great-aunt Helena—my father's aunt—lived there. She lived alone, with a grand piano and a small, fluffy white dog, a Maltese. I was too young to get the story straight, but I had some idea that when she was young, during the war, she'd escaped from a convent and hidden from enemy soldiers. Her house seemed extravagant to me, full of velvets, with beautiful, draped curtains. Every sofa was covered with huge elaborately dressed dolls that we weren't allowed to touch. My aunt sewed fancy dresses for everyone in town, and she herself dressed like a silent movie star, in stylish hats and fancy shoes.

When I was three or four years old, my twin cousins, who were about my age, lived on the second floor of our house, which was built to be a duplex. My great-aunt, who had gone to conservatory in Ukraine, started teaching the three of us piano. She would show us something, then we would take turns trying it out.

Around that time, my mother and aunt signed me and my cousins up for a preschool that specialized in music. We played instruments, sang, and learned kid-level music theory. After a year, my cousins decided they didn't want to do it anymore, but I loved it. I entered my first piano competition when I was almost five. We took a train to a nearby town—my first train ride—and when I signed in, I could barely write my first name. But I won a prize in my age group, and from then on, my life was filled with traveling from one competition to another.

A few years later, Aunt Helena was dying. She had cancer, but because that word was taboo my parents said she had trouble with her stomach. My mother told me that she was asking for me to play "Lullaby for Bear," a very simple song she'd taught me. The piano was in the corner of her bedroom. I was only five or six—I didn't understand death—but I played, and every time I finished, she said, "Magda, play it again."

The mentality people in my community had at the time was that every child was expected to specialize in something—maybe it was a Russian thing. One of my sisters played cello. She was very talented, but a bit lazy. One of my brothers was a genius in biology, winning science competitions all over the country. Once piano was determined to be my talent, I spent the rest of my childhood focused on it. I went to school in the morning, then home for lunch, then to music school all afternoon. There was no school bus and my mother was too busy to drive me, so I walked almost four miles a day, rain, snow, or shine. Sometimes I would catch the town bus, but waiting for it might take twenty minutes.

It was never worth it, so in addition to my full school schedule, I spent about two hours a day commuting by foot. If I had a math test, I would wake up at 3:00 a.m. to study for it.

When a competition was coming up, the music school would write a letter excusing me from regular school. Then sometimes they'd lock us in a practice room for eight hours a day. Some kids would jump out of the second-floor window onto the grassy yard and sneak into town. I'd look out and see my friends waving. "Come on Magda, let's go!" It was tempting, but I never joined them. I was afraid of heights.

It's ironic that Nathaniel's ears were the first problem I noticed, and I can't even claim that it was the fear that he would live in a world without music. Truthfully, all I cared about in those first moments of ignorance and shock was his appearance — and that's what many people still think is most important when they see him. However, by the time he was a week old, I understood that his looks, his missing ears, his hearing — these were at the bottom of the list of my worries.

When he was only a few months old, Dr. Bernstein pushed us to get him a hearing aid. Though he had no outer ears to channel noise, just a tiny flap of skin, his inner ear was fine. He was a great candidate for a bone-anchored hearing aid (a BAHA), which carries sound vibrations directly through your bone to your inner ear. At first, it would be held on his head by a tight rubber band. Later, it would be mounted into his skull.

There were good reasons to wait until he was older to introduce this hearing aid. A big one was cost. Insurance puts hearing aids in the category of "durable medical equipment," which meant they were only reimbursable up to $500. At the time, the BAHA cost $5,000. Yeah, not great. (The price of the most expensive BAHAs has gone up to $7,000, but now some insurance companies cover 80 percent of the cost.) We learned that the longer a child goes without being able to hear well, the more difficulty he has learning to speak. The earlier we gave him sound, the better shot he had at talking normally.

We followed Dr. Bernstein's advice and scheduled Nathaniel to get his BAHA when he was still only a few months old. Russel and I met the hearing specialist in the audiology room at NYU. The doctor told us, "Some babies get upset because they're not used to such loud noises around them. We'll try it for two minutes, and if he cries we'll take it off."

The doctor handed me the hearing aid and showed me how to turn it on. When I first put it on him, Nathaniel started fussing, as if to say, "What are you doing to my head?" The headband that held it in place had to be really tight.

Then I turned it on. We didn't know what to expect, but as soon as we spoke quietly to him, Nathaniel's face lit up. His eyes got big. He smiled and looked around with happy curiosity.

He started babbling and looked startled at the sound of his own voice. His face brightened, and he babbled more. Everything about his expression said, "This is a miracle." Russel started crying, as he is wont to do.

Then, because the doctor didn't want to overstimulate him, I took the hearing aid off. The corners of Nathaniel's mouth immediately turned down. He reached toward me. He wanted it back!

I suddenly felt grateful. To hear was a gift, like every sense, one of the miracles of life that most of us experience every day. Seeing the joy on my son's face made me realize how much I took my own hearing for granted.

From that moment on Nathaniel did not want to take his BAHA off. Ever. If we tried, he'd start crying. He eventually got used to the idea that it had to come off for sleeping and bathing, but as soon as he woke up or finished a bath, he'd look around for it and make it clear that he wanted it back. Now I had to add a backup battery to the list of supplies I carried at all times. When the battery died, he'd cry and point to his hearing aid. Heaven help us if we were on a long car trip when it died. If I didn't have a battery on hand, we were in for a long, loud tantrum while we detoured to find the closest drugstore.

Later, when Nathaniel was around two and a half and potty training, his hearing aid accidentally fell in the toilet. That's right, the $5,000 hearing aid that was so sensitive to moisture that he couldn't even wear it out in the rain. The stretchy headband that held it on tended to loosen over time and occasionally needed to be replaced, and it must have been pretty stretched out to fall off at this inopportune moment. Nathaniel was horrified—he knew what a disaster this was. He immediately started wailing, "I want my hearing aid!"

Thankfully I was there with him in the bathroom. In one of my least favorite—but still heroic—moments, I reached into the toilet full of pee and grabbed the hearing aid. I quickly swiped it with a disinfectant wipe and dropped it into the dehumidifying container where it ordinarily lived at night. Three hours later, it was miraculously restored.

We called the BAHA his "magic ear." With it, a new world of sound opened to him. He could hear dogs barking. Birds singing. Kids playing. Cars driving by. He reacted to everything. Before, when he watched TV, he had sat silently. It hadn't occurred to me that he might do anything different. But now, when he watched Baby Einstein or heard me play the piano or listened to the Wiggles, he danced and sang. And when he was still being fed for hours through the g-tube, I could put on a video and know that he wasn't bored out of his mind. He became a much happier child.

When you're taking care of a baby twenty-four hours a day, every new thing they do is miraculous. That's why every mom thinks her child is a genius — because she watched the baby go from doing nothing but eat and sleep to smiling, clapping, and learning to speak a whole language pretty fluently in just a few years. My baby's milestones were skewed, but I know that when Nathaniel got his hearing aid, his personality came alive. I lived for his expressions and joy.

## 10. division of labor

My whole life was devoted to Nathaniel, and it was a problem. Fall passed, winter came again, and in February Nathaniel would turn one. With all of his equipment, it was hard to leave the house. I had hoped that as time passed and I learned how to take care of him, things would get easier, but some of my darkest hours, literally and figuratively, were the winter I spent in that Long Island basement. Hal was kind to renovate for us, but the one thing he couldn't fix was the small, high basement windows. Every morning Hal, Nancy, and Russel would head off to work. I'd watch them go then retreat to the basement. There was no natural light. My life revolved around feeding Nathaniel constantly. He was a delightful, mellow baby and my best buddy. I'd read him books and tell him stories, or he'd play with his trains. But he spent hours hooked up to his feeding bags, and I was hooked to him. We were trapped and isolated.

Things would brighten when Jenna and Emily came to visit. Even though it was cold, we would bundle up the babies, put them on the swing set, and talk about Emily's experience in preschool. It was going well, and it gave me hope for Nathaniel.

It is horrible to say and disturbing to me that it's true, but I almost fainted when I saw Emily for the first time. She didn't have a trach, but her features were so small, fragile, and close together that it was shocking. How silly and embarrassing this is, but I admit it because it's important for all of us to acknowledge that, no matter how rationally inclusive and just we are, we're still subject to physiological reactions that we can't control. Even now, after all I have experienced, I might still have that reaction. It says nothing about Emily and everything about me. That should make anyone feel better about how they might react: If I can have this reaction, anyone can. The best I can do is try to handle myself with grace.

In Hoboken I had rented a piano and had a few students. We brought the piano to the basement, and I was now teaching Hal and Nancy's twelve-year-old daughter, Chelsey, and one other student. I had played for Nathaniel from the beginning, mostly to keep myself sane. He'd sit on my lap and I knew he could hear a little of it and that he definitely felt the vibrations. Now that he could hear clearly, I selected my music more deliberately: Bach, because it is very mathematically constructed. Debussy, which is more like impressionist painting. I picked a few pieces to play over and over so he would learn to recognize them. Nathaniel loved Debussy's "Arabesque." He had connected to me through music even before he had his hearing aid, but it made all the difference to see his face respond. Russel still talks about how it lifted all of our spirits.

I loved playing the piano, especially for Nathaniel, but as my only escape, it wasn't enough. The more adept I got at managing Nathaniel's various tubes and gizmos, the less possible it seemed that there was anyone else who could stay with him to give me a break. There was Russel and his mother, Barbara, who now knew how to suction Nathaniel too. But otherwise I just wasn't comfortable leaving him for any period of time. Ever since the nurse had displaced his stent, I had a hard time trusting my son's care to anyone else.

Anxiety over Nathaniel's special needs wasn't the only reason I was so dedicated to him. It's how I was raised. In America, parenting culture tends to revolve around the idea that everyone has their own path. Children live with their parents, who love and care for them while looking for ways to nurture their own interests and/or careers. Reasonable enough, but in our little Polish village, my mother—and even my father—made providing for us their life's purpose. As hard as my mother worked in the garden and on the farm, she came home in the middle of each day to cook us lunch. After school, both parents would sit with us around the kitchen table, and my mother would sip coffee and ask, "How was your day? Do you have homework?"

Dad would say, "I'm going fishing this afternoon; does anybody have time to join me?" Some of us would go, some wouldn't.

Before I became a parent, I had career opportunities. I could have been a music professor, but I don't say that wistfully. Now my priority was to care for Nathaniel and to do everything I could to give him a happy childhood. I deliberately dropped having a life of my own outside of being his mother. I struggled, but I chose to struggle—so it was all me, always, twenty-four hours a day. We were tied to each other. Most of my day was dedicated to Nathaniel, then I'd prepare dinner for the household.

I'd grown up cooking with my mother and had always loved it. Polish food is designed to take as long as possible to prepare. You have to fry or bake each ingredient separately, then combine them and cook them again. Many recipes require homemade dough, which makes the whole ordeal take forever. Pierogis, stuffed cabbage, and pickles are all delicious, but they take hours to make. In Poland, many women stay home to feed their families, and traditional Polish food does its best to keep it that way. Or maybe the women invented complex recipes to make staying home more interesting. It's a chicken/egg situation, or in Poland it would be a pierogi/golabki situation. Nowadays women are coming out of their kitchens and ditching some of these recipes. I don't cook many Polish meals now because they're not very nutritious, and I learned long ago that there are better ways to spend my time. Given the choice, I'd rather take a nap!

But when I was living in the basement, even preparing the foods I loved was unrewarding. I took responsibility for dinner because I wanted to show my gratitude to Hal and Nancy. It was no surprise that everyone was tired when they came home from work, especially Russel after his epic commute. The problem was that I was eager—okay desperate—to talk to adults. But they had been dealing with adults all day long and were spent by the time we sat down. They would quietly eat what I cooked, then move to the couch to watch TV for the rest of the evening. I felt like I was there to serve everyone else.

That feeling wasn't confined to mealtime. I had no time, no money, no friends, no freedom, no life, nothing. It was like I didn't exist. Alone with the baby in my brother-in-law's basement, I felt like I was losing my mind. My body was worn down from lack of sleep and stress from constantly monitoring Nathaniel to make sure he didn't pull out his trach or g-tube. Then, when he was sleeping, I held his hand so I could tell if he moved. If he started fussing, I checked to see if the trach was in. Crawling around after him, watching him like a hawk, I could never relax.

I was miserable. I was jealous of my sister-in-law's career and seemingly normal, balanced life. Every day Nancy dressed nicely, put Chelsey on the bus, and went to work. Sometimes she had dinner with friends or went shopping for clothes. I couldn't remember the last time I put on something nice to wear, and it felt like my brain was deteriorating.

The only time Nathaniel and I left the basement was to go to the grocery store. I still hadn't managed to get a driver's license. My hometown, as with most of Poland, was designed to be navigated by public transportation, by bicycle, or on foot. It couldn't have been more different from Long Island, where you needed a car to go almost everywhere.

The closest supermarket was two miles away, just about the distance I had walked to school growing up. I would put Nathaniel in a stroller, bundle us both up, pack the trach pump, and walk to the supermarket no matter the weather, staying on the sidewalk when there was one and moving to the street when there wasn't. Eventually I found a shortcut through a neighbor's field. I remember pushing Nathaniel across the field during winter and looking back to see the stroller tracks cutting through the snow, like a strange animal had come out of hibernation and gone looking for food. After shopping, I'd bring the groceries home stuffed in the storage basket underneath the stroller.

I cried every single day, pitying myself, and aching for Nathaniel. I still couldn't accept the fact that this was real, and I still had dreams that it was just that—a dream. I was forgetting to eat and dropped too much weight. When we drove into Manhattan I had a vision of opening the passenger door, jumping out of the car, and being hit by another car. I was scaring myself.

Russel was worried about me. My English still wasn't great,

so he found me a Polish psychiatrist who listened to me describe what was going on, and confirmed that I was clinically depressed. He put me on 50 milligrams of Zoloft, a hefty dose.

I stopped crying, but I also became like wood. When I watched TV, I didn't react. It felt as if there was a pane of glass between me and the rest of the world. The medication took me from one extreme to another—from being too emotional to not feeling anything at all.

I'd been on Zoloft for four months or so when I thought of a moment from my childhood that told me exactly what I needed. My uncle Eligiusz, who was a ranger in our area, had a big forest behind his house. Every Sunday after church we'd go there for a big family lunch, then my brother, sister, cousins, and I would play together for hours. We'd make houses in the woods out of sheets and sticks, climb trees, and make mud soup with flower petal spices. Every once in a while in the evening, my uncle would make a fire in the backyard and roast kielbasa.

At one of those nighttime gatherings, Uncle Eligiusz said, "I have something to show you guys." He led a parade of kids by flashlight into the woods. Coming to an open grassy area, he pulled aside a clump of leaves to reveal a mother hedgehog, with a bunch of pink-skinned newborn babies. I was in awe, realizing how often we ran among the trees, unaware of what creatures were right under foot.

My uncle said, "You have to keep your eyes open. There are secret worlds all around us."

A few things hit me about that story. First, I wanted a childhood like that for Nathaniel, one where he could run freely in the woods, making his own fun from scratch. That was something I'd always wanted for my children. What I realized was that I was like that mother hedgehog. I'd been hiding with my son underground, taking shelter in a safe bubble, protecting him when he was most vulnerable. Nobody would get to us. No illness, no accidents. And nobody knew we were there.

Second, I thought about the people in the outside world, how they might pass our hiding place day after day without ever knowing we were there. In our safety was isolation, and the same is true for every family in every house that any of us pass, the secrets and suffering and nurturing kept underground. We don't know each other. If we want to share our vastly different worlds, if we want to connect, we have to come out sometime.

It was time for Nathaniel and me to emerge from that protected darkness into the sunny real world.

I was ready.


The first Christmas after Russel and I met, he made his second trip to Poland since our summer in the Hamptons had ended. This time he bought a one-way ticket with plans to stay for around six weeks.

I told Russel all about our beautiful farm before he came to visit, but to his mind the reality didn't live up to my romantic memories. Outside, he expected to see shiny glass greenhouses harboring the fresh vegetables I'd described, but ours were in disrepair, with broken glass, grayed-out windows, rusted metal columns, and vines weaving in and out of the windows. I shrugged off his surprise. I'd never known anything else.

The first thing he noticed when he walked into the house was that everyone in my family was wearing pajamas, robes, and down parkas inside the house. To this day, there's no modern heat, just a coal furnace and a wood stove, and when it gets really cold, my father adjusts the heat vents to direct them toward the *greenhouse* so the tomatoes don't freeze. The colder it is outside, the colder it is inside. My wimpy American boyfriend was perpetually shivering, even with his coat on.

That evening, Russel was so cold he couldn't sleep. Although I enjoyed watching the city boy suffer a little, I'm not heartless, so I dug up an old space heater. Halfway through the night, I woke up to the smell of an electrical fire. The heater had shorted. Russel thought the house was seconds from burning down.

The second night, he shook me out of a deep sleep. "Wake up! What's that noise?" He thought there was an animal trying to claw its way through the wall.

"Go back to sleep," I told him. "That's just my father refilling the furnace."

Three weeks earlier he had been serving cocktails to Mariah Carey and her entourage in the Hamptons. Now he was listening to the unfamiliar sound of someone shoveling coal into a furnace in Sanok, Poland. He told me he loved it. And me.

At some point on that trip, we were driving with my father in his tiny, rickety red car, with five-speed manual transmission, ripped seats, windows you could barely crank, and no heat. Most likely we were going fishing.

Russel turned to me and, speaking in English, which he knew my father wouldn't understand, said, "Hey, if we're going to get married, I should probably ask your dad first."

I turned to my father and translated, "Russel thinks he needs to ask you if he can marry me."

My father shrugged, as if to say, "Sure, why not?"

Russel said, "What did you just do? Tell me you didn't ask your father just now." That was exactly what I had done. He asked, "So, are we getting married?"

I replied, "Yeah!"

There was no formal proposal. No getting down on one knee. That night we went to midnight mass. As was traditional, we each had a shot of vodka before braving the cold drive to a tiny church one town away. It was dark and quiet outside. The building was barn-like and covered with a fresh foot of snow. Inside, it was brightly lit, there was a fire, and it was full of people. The scene was magical, even for someone who's not religious. The service was all in Polish, but Russel was mesmerized. And cold. As far as I could tell, he was cold every minute he spent in Poland. As we left the church, Russel said, "I really do want to marry you."

I said, "Yes, I really want to marry you too."

The week between Christmas and New Year's, I introduced him to all of my family. There are thirty cousins, six uncles, and seven aunts, all of whom wanted Russel to share the vodka that they'd made in their basements. He wanted to be polite, and that meant he was drunk the entire time.

On New Year's Day I woke up early and went down to the kitchen. There was a breakfast nook with an old wooden table, a stove with wood stacked next to it, a teapot on the stove, and coffee brewing. The table was spread with a typical continental breakfast: cheese, meats, bread. A little while later Russel, hungover again, came down to eat.

My English still wasn't great, but I knew how to tell him this: "You know I'm not marrying a bartender, right?"

Russel was taken aback. "What? You said yes! We're getting married."

I said, "Yes, we're getting married. When you get a better job. Here's the deal: I get my masters on June 28. Two weeks before that day, if you've found another job, I will give up my life here, get on a plane, come to the US, and marry you. If you don't have a job, I'm not coming."

Russel took my ultimatum seriously, but he flew back to post-9/11 New York and couldn't even get an interview. In desperation, he called an old college buddy who was working in insurance and said, "Hey Bill, I'm desperate. I need a job. Can we at least have lunch?"

They met for a drink and Russel said, "I've got this gorgeous concert pianist from Eastern Europe who's willing to marry me." Apparently, he pulled out my photo to show him. He went on. "The only problem is if I don't have a job she won't."

Bill replied, "I'm getting you a job at Chubb."

He was true to his word, and Russel got a job as an operations manager with one month to spare. As promised, I booked my flight.

We were both holding up our ends of the bargain, but I had spent over a year in that basement, a pump on one arm and a feeding bag on the other. I was skinny, fragile, and hunched over as I maneuvered Nathaniel from one doctor's appointment to another. When I told Russel I needed to get out, he didn't question me.

We saved every paycheck, survived on Hal and Nancy's generosity, managed to pay off some of the medical bills, and our credit score clawed its way back up. Finally, after eight months in the basement, Russel told me we had enough money saved to buy a house in Charlotte. His company was willing to relocate him to North Carolina, with a promotion no less, and his parents were building a house in the area. This was a light at the end of the tunnel.

*part two*

## a normal childhood

# 11. a house of our own

It was spring and Nathaniel was a little over a year old when we moved to North Carolina. Packing for Hal's basement, we had fit everything we owned in a pickup truck: a mattress, a box spring, and a couple of dressers from Russel's bachelorhood. But in the past year we'd acquired a crib, some toys, and an impressive cache of medical equipment and supplies, so this time we hired a small moving truck that, though it had a head start on us, would arrive a couple days after we did.

The highway from Long Island to Charlotte threaded through rural Pennsylvania. Russel drove—I had failed my driver's test some embarrassing number of times because I could not parallel park for the life of me—and I was happy to be the passenger, watching the blurred world speed past. We were above ground. We were free.

All of Charlotte was in bloom. Our house was in a new, cookie-cutter development, the kind where all the houses look the same and there's a single, sad tree that looks like it's ten years away from providing shade quivering weakly in every front yard. The previous owners had forgotten to take some garlic out of the fridge, but aside from the terrible smell, the place was in good shape. I gave the entire house a scrub-down with white vinegar, my mother's favorite natural disinfectant. The sun blazed through the windows, and I could feel it working magic on me. I had never been so grateful for windows.

We would drive back to New York for Nathaniel's appointments every couple of months—we couldn't afford to fly—but Nathaniel would have a break after one more big surgery, so we would be able to settle into a routine. The feeling of barely surviving gradually faded. A family doctor helped me wean myself off Zoloft, and I started trying to give my now-walking boy not just food and air but a real childhood.

Growing up on a farm defined my childhood. We had a huge yard with three glass greenhouses and three foil greenhouses. Inside were tomatoes, cucumbers, and lettuce. Outside were plots of carrots, potatoes, parsley, Brussels sprouts, berries, and a grove of walnut trees. In the spring and summer, we grew roses and white, purple, and light pink mums that my father sold to local florists. People put the mums on the graves of those they loved for All Saints' Day. The farm was full of color, smells, and creatures: an enchanted paradise.

Given the wonders right outside our back door, I didn't have or want many toys: there was a cloth doll that someone had made for me, and my brother had a few toy cars. Maybe there were some blocks. One summer my father went to America to try to earn money to replace our beat-up car, which we needed to bring the fruits and vegetables to the market. On a three-month travel visa, he ended up working as a gardener for some wealthy people in the Hamptons for a year.

It was 1989, and while he was away, Communism started to fall in Poland and, with it, the exchange rate. The money he brought back suddenly wasn't even close to being enough for a car, but he did bring me a Barbie doll. She wore a blue leotard with a pink belt and had long blonde hair. I was very excited to have her, but my few hard-won toys didn't mean as much to me as the wonderland that was right outside our back door. My fantasies of child-raising were about the backyard I'd played in as a child and the woods beyond it. I wanted my children to experience the same exploration and wonder that sparked my imagination at a young age.

I always planned to have lots of kids. As the oldest of six, I was always helping out with my siblings. My brother Michal, the fourth-born, is fifteen years younger than I am. Even though I went to music school every day after regular high school, after Michal was born I hurried home in between to see him. When I wasn't home, my mother brought Michal with her everywhere, to weed the garden, to pick tomatoes. She'd lug a hand-me-down Exer-Saucer around with her and let him bounce and watch. When I took over, I immediately pushed his stroller into the woods. We'd off-road it, bumping the stroller over tree roots and through gullies. This was our routine for the first few years of his life. I'd point to knotholes in the trees and tell him, "This is where the elves live. They go down through the tree to their underground world." Then I'd kneel next to him and say, "Oh my God, I just saw a little elf! Did you see it scamper back into the tree? They're so fast!"

Michal would say, "Oh yes, I saw his little hat."

Michal is only eleven years older than Nathaniel, so in some ways Nathaniel felt like my second baby. No matter what his constraints, I wanted to explore the world with him just like I had with my little brother.

Our backyard in Charlotte had a patio and a sunny patch where Nathaniel and I planted a flower garden. Beyond the garden was a steep hill, at the top of which was a muddy play area. Every morning I brought my coffee to the top of the hill and slowly sipped it while Nathaniel played in the dirt with his trains and Tonka trucks. Making up stories about construction vehicles wasn't exactly scintillating, but the warm, sunny mornings in the fresh air were exactly what I needed. Our neighborhood had a playground and a kiddie pool. This was Nathaniel's first pool, and though I had to be very careful his trach didn't get wet, he absolutely loved swimming.

Our life in North Carolina started to take shape. A few months after we moved, I finally passed my driver's test, which opened up our world even more. We only had one car, so some days I would drop off Russel at work and then drive Nathaniel to story-time at the bookstore. There was a Thomas the Tank Engine table there where he was content to play for hours.

Nathaniel had come to love Thomas trains after his first jaw distraction, back in Long Island. After that first surgery, Nathaniel had to sit still for hours while nutrients slowly made their way through the g-tube into his body. His train table became his salvation. He got a new train or two after every surgery, and he had spent countless hours like that, slowly being fed and playing with the trains. Now he was thrilled to find his favorite hobby out in the world.

He wasn't the only Thomas-obsessed kid, so he made a couple of "train" friends (the children's version of poker buddies), and the mothers and I would smile at each other, sometimes exchanging sympathetic words about the brain-numbing effects of trains that speak but are otherwise plot-challenged.

In the evenings, when Russel and I cooked together, Nathaniel was perched in his high chair, eating alongside us. He still had a g-tube, but he was barely using it now. We kept it, as many Treacher Collins families do, in anticipation of emergencies or future jaw surgeries that might make it difficult for him to eat.

Every life comes with its own limitations and advantages: When I was young, mine were driven by where and when I was growing up. I'll never forget the first Snickers bar that made it to our farm. I was six. We split it among all the cousins, and it was the best thing I'd ever tasted. No chocolate, rationed meat, a government that told us what our careers would be . . . none of this was upsetting because it was normal to me, my siblings, and everyone we knew.

Maybe "normal" is leading the same life as everyone around you, enjoying the same luxuries, encountering similar hardships. In the Long Island basement, I had felt isolated, chained by my difference. Feeling sorry for oneself comes from thinking you have it harder, that you've been dealt a worse hand, or that you somehow deserve a better one. But we can all look around and see both worse and better. We all, at some point, have to come to peace with our place on the spectrum. Russel and I struggled with this, the "why us?" of it all, and maybe we always will, but in Charlotte, for the first time I began to step back from that, coming to terms with the struggles and joys Nathaniel was bringing me, and trying to feel grateful and blessed at the same time.

Settling in Charlotte gave me the mental space to want a second child. Not only was I starting to get the hang of Nathaniel, but I had a few somewhat selfish reasons: First, I wanted

Nathaniel to have a guardian angel, someone to protect him when I couldn't. Second, I was afraid Nathaniel would never have children, so I would never have grandchildren. God knows how or why I was looking so far ahead, but there was no way I wanted to miss out on being a grandmother. Finally, maybe it was just the way I was raised, but I expected my children to take care of me when I got old. Being an only child to aging parents is a lot of responsibility, and I was nervous about putting that much pressure on one child.

Most of all, however, I wanted to have at least two kids so they could play with each other. When I was growing up, spending time with my siblings was one of my greatest joys. I'd thought about that ever since Jenna brought Emily to visit us in the basement. She'd also brought her second child, a newborn, and said how glad she was to have children close in age. She told me it was hard, but she was confident the reward would come later: They would always have each other.

For all my rationalizing, the simple truth was I just wanted another baby.

But there was one concern that we had to address: We didn't want another child with Treacher Collins. It wasn't that we couldn't or wouldn't love a second child with the condition—there was more than enough love in our hearts. What we didn't have was the time, money, or emotional bandwidth. To give another child as much medical attention as Nathaniel required would have been too much for all of us.

Treacher Collins is a genetic mutation that presents along a continuum. On one end, a child might be born with droopy eyes, reduced cheekbones, and a smaller jaw, but nothing that causes medical issues. It gets worse with every generation that the gene is passed down, and we've even met parents who didn't know they had the mutation until they gave birth to a child with it. Even though Nathaniel was a first generation Treacher Collins child, he didn't have a mild case. Whatever could go wrong had gone wrong, and we didn't want to take chances it could happen again.

The next time we drove up to NYU for a meeting with Nathaniel's whole team—ENT, craniofacial specialist, psychologist, dental team, and pediatrician—we asked to meet with a geneticist to talk about a second child.

I was open about my concerns. "I want to try for another child," I said, "but I'm scared."

The geneticist ordered blood samples from me, Russel, and Nathaniel, but he told me that the only way to really find out if my next embryo would have Treacher Collins would be to get pregnant. And so I did.

Early in the pregnancy I had a chorionic villus sampling (CVS), a prenatal test that identifies chromosomal or genetic disorders in a fetus. It was nerve-wracking. Nathaniel and Russel waited outside the exam room door for me. We were hoping for a definitive answer, but although the test didn't detect the mutation, the doctors wouldn't make any promises. Whether we liked it or not, we would have to wait until the fetus grew more and they could do a detailed sonogram. Then, if it had Treacher Collins, we would have to decide whether to keep it or abort. We knew we had that option, but I couldn't say whether I would take it.

Sometimes people ask me what I would have done if I'd known early on about the problems Nathaniel would have. (People are actually surprisingly bold in asking this question.) Now that 3D and 4D sonograms are available, Treacher Collins is identified early in pregnancies, but back then, a fetus would have been too far along to terminate before any test could diagnose it. But if I'm playing the "if" game: If I'd known in advance and had time to process that the baby had problems, I would have seriously considered continuing the pregnancy. I'm pro-choice, but it would have been hard for me to let go of a fetus if it was likely to survive. Knowing the good and bad in advance — that he would have severe issues, but that there was nothing wrong with his internal organs — I would have had time to prepare myself mentally and emotionally, research the syndrome, and line up the best doctors. The hardest part by far had been the initial shock of Nathaniel's birth. When life takes a sudden, unexpected turn, we are asked to show what we are made of. But now — with perspective — I am astounded when I think about how much of the trauma was due to the surprise.

As I considered a second pregnancy, I was still a new mom, still recovering from the day of Nathaniel's birth, and Nathaniel needed me 100 percent of the time. There was no way I could handle another child with similar needs. Russel and I were in agreement on this: We wanted to have as "normal" a parenting experience as possible. Emotionally, neither of us could watch a child go through what Nathaniel had again. If we could avoid bringing another child into the world who had to deal with the challenges he faced, we would. And — this is the most important part — Nathaniel agrees. Like many a first child, the last thing he wanted was to sacrifice his parents' undivided attention.

I feel differently now, though. I'm older and more mature, and practically an expert on Treacher Collins. Both my boys are strong and independent, and there are so many more resources and new technologies available to families like ours. I can assuredly say that I could and would care for a baby with severe issues all over again. The person I was when Nathaniel was born would be astounded by the person I am now.

At six months, I had a 4D ultrasound that measured the fetus's head, jaw, and ears. We could clearly see his features. An ear! The most noticeable trait in Treacher Collins is the malformed ear. The doctors still wouldn't make any guarantees, but when I saw that ear I knew deep in my heart that this baby was okay.

Looking back, I remember being worried when I saw the ultrasounds of Nathaniel. These were standard ultrasounds, not the 3D and 4D ones they do nowadays. But in them, his nose looked disproportionately big for a baby. I told myself I was being ridiculous; I was a first-time mom, what did I know? Now, after having my concerns validated, I had stronger faith in my intuition, and my intuition told me not to worry about my second son.

In our family, the fact that our second son would be genetically "normal" meant that he was going to need less, and that he was going to get less. That would be his blessing and burden.

*Nathaniel: What is normal? Maybe "normal" is what is possible. If someone could fly, it wouldn't be normal because nobody else could do it. But nobody can fly, so nobody is abnormal. But nobody's normal because everyone's different. So "normal" only applies to minor, earthly things. Nothing as cool as being able to fly. Who wants that?*

*If people don't see me as normal, they're only seeing a tiny piece of me — the outside, from the neck up. But normal isn't better. Flying isn't normal, but it's better than walking. Having four dogs isn't normal, but it's better than three. Then again, I'm biased because I have four dogs.*

A few weeks before the 4D sonogram, we had gone in to meet with our local doctor, a very well-known and respected ENT we saw for breathing issues and emergencies. He looked at Nathaniel's CT scan, the structure of his face, his muscles, and his bones, and said, "All my life I've done impossible things. I can do this. I can fix his airway and remove the trach." He was utterly confident.

Nathaniel was two years old and the tracheostomy was his biggest constraint. The longer you keep a trach in, the longer you are dependent on it, and the more likely it is that you will have it for the rest of your life. From the very beginning, our overall goal was to get rid of it, and the sooner the better. Think of it: You don't see a lot of people walking around with trachs. You don't see doctors, teachers, waiters, judges—few people  out there in the world, leading so-called normal lives and having normal careers—with a trach. On first meeting, people often assumed that our primary concern was Nathaniel's appearance, but Russel and I weren't worried about that in the least. For a long time he had just looked like himself to us, our sweet baby. What we wanted was for him to breathe without help. We wanted him to be free.

We called our doctors at NYU to ask what they thought about this new doctor and his proposal. They said that he was known to be a wonderful surgeon, and it was possible that he might have success where they had struggled. Dr. Bernstein had already tried to remove the trach three separate times, starting after Nathaniel's first jaw distraction. Each time he tried, he had gone into the operating room with Nathaniel, and had come right back out fifteen minutes later. He'd say, "The bone is thicker than I thought, and it's close to his brain. I can't do it."

Now Dr. Bernstein and our other doctors encouraged us to let the Charlotte doctor give it a try.

. . .

Just before the surgery, the doctor came out to the room where Russel and I were waiting. For some reason I noticed that he was wearing a white turtleneck under his scrubs.

"Let's pray to Jesus Christ, so he guides my hand in the right direction," he said, reaching for our hands. Russel and I looked at each other. I don't like to mix religion and science, and I had never encountered a doctor who did, but there was no harm in being operated on by a good Christian man.

Russel said, "Praying never hurt."

"From your mouth to God's ears," I said.

In the town where I grew up there were more churches than supermarkets. My parents were devout Catholics, and we went to church every Sunday morning. If I asked to sleep in (which I did), my parents made me go to services by myself in the afternoon. To be honest, I never liked church. It was the same thing over and over again, and they made you feel like everything you did was bad. As a teenager, I'd bring a Discman and hide in the back of the church where the organ player was. During the mass, while the priest rambled on about politics and how much money the church needed, I'd listen to music. Every Sunday the priest served Communion, and if you didn't take a wafer, you were a sinner. Then there was confession. If I *didn't* come up with any sins to confess, then in the church's eyes I was a sinner, so I made up sins: "I lied to my mom. I told her I ate three pound cakes but I really ate two." And then my sin was lying in confession. It didn't make sense to me. The priest lived in a monastery with ten other men. They didn't have wives or children. None of this added up to me. How and why were they experts on how we should live? But I believed in God and spoke to him often, and, my misgivings about

Communion and confession aside, I liked the commitment and ritual of going to church.

Back in that little gastropub in Prague, when Russel and I had written down the names Nathaniel and Jakub, the question of religion had come up. "I know so much about Catholicism," I said, "and it was a big part of my life growing up. I'd like our kids to be Catholic."

Russel, who was raised in a secular Jewish family, countered, "I want them to learn about Judaism too."

"But you didn't practice as much as I did," I said. "Your parents didn't go to services once a week." For Russel, those rituals weren't as important as his Jewish identity, which was part of his daily life.

I suggested a compromise. "We both believe in one god, we just acknowledge it differently. Let's have God decide. If our first child is a boy, let's raise him and the rest of our children Jewish. I'll do everything in my power to learn about your religion and to raise our children to follow it. And if God gives us a daughter, that means he decided we should raise all our kids Catholic."

Russel agreed. "Okay, we'll have God decide." And we truly believed that God would take care of this decision for us.

When we found out we were having a boy, I was in shock for a couple of days. I would be leaving my religion behind. My children wouldn't go to church, and my family and others in my hometown would fear for their souls. But I reminded myself that most religions come back to one god, with different ways of showing devotion. I didn't feel a need to decide that one way was better than another.

In Poland we say, "The world is a theater. God is a director. You are an actor." It's okay that I don't know in advance what the play is about. God is directing me. Anyway, if God is the director, he cast my children as Jews.

When we found out the baby was going to be a boy and therefore a Jew, we joined a temple in Hoboken and went to couples' classes on Judaism twice a week until Nathaniel was born. I came to love how Judaism contemplates the big questions—the nature of God, the universe, life, death, why we are here, why bad things happen—without requiring you to believe in specific answers. Instead of being focused on the status of your soul, Judaism emphasizes ethics in daily life. Humans have freedom of choice, and we can choose obedience or disobedience, but God never wants to break his covenant with us—the promise to protect us—and so if we fail, we can always return to him. In Catholicism, by contrast, there is a right choice or a wrong choice. They tell you the right choice, and that's what you're supposed to do or you end up in Purgatory. Russel and I attended those classes for fun and enlightenment, oblivious to how soon we would be at God's doorstep, questioning him and asking for guidance.

Three hours passed while the doctor worked on Nathaniel. This seemed promising, as Dr. Bernstein had always come out of the OR so quickly with the news that he couldn't do anything. I was thinking, *Oh my God, it's happening! He's going to be successful!*

Finally the doctor emerged, white as a ghost. He sat us down in a private room and said, "I am very sorry, my hand slipped. I went too far. I poked your son's brain with the drill. I made a hole. His brain fluid is leaking through his nose."

"Your. Hand. Slipped." Russel was incredulous. What happened to Jesus Christ steering it? Had this doctor put a little too much medical responsibility in Jesus's hands?

He explained that they had filled the hole and put two feet of bandages into Nathaniel's nose.

"Is he going to be brain damaged?" I asked the doctor.

"I just don't know," he said. "If bacteria got in the brain, anything is possible."

I did not take this news calmly. My first thought was, *I'm not going to get my son back. I'm going to get a vegetable back.* I went into shock, literally pulling fistfuls of hair from my head. I don't know how I did it; I must have pulled really hard.

Nathaniel was the one with the medical issues, but every time he had surgery, Russel and I had our own emotional struggles. Most people had some concept of this. "It must be so hard on you," they would say. But it was more than that. It was stressful, exhausting, and enduring. Hair pulling had become my response to the most stressful situations, and while Russel had his hair-pulling moments too, more often he would punch the walls. What a pair we were.

When Nathaniel came out of the OR he was still unconscious. I lay down on the bed next to him, holding his hand and wailing loudly, imagining him waking up and not knowing who I was.

Finally, he opened his eyes. He took one look at my face, stroked my back, and said, "It's okay, Mommy." And it was. At least for him. My turn was next.

They sent him home after a week in the hospital, instructing me, "Keep looking to see if something is leaking from his nose."

Pondering a lawsuit sometime later, Russel requested the surgical notes. That's how we found out how serious the situation had been. Apparently, before the surgeon emerged from the OR to tell us what he had done, the operating room had gone into emergency mode, with a neurosurgeon running in to plug

Nathaniel's leaking skull with a waxy rubber substance. It was literally like a cork, and it was extremely important that it stay in place for an indefinite period of time. In every surgery Nathaniel would have for the next *eight years*, the surgeon would have to take care not to dislodge the plug. They would literally map a way to avoid that area because, as it turns out, poking a hole in someone's skull is a big deal.

Russel also noticed an interesting detail about the doctor's method in the notes. Ordinarily in surgeries requiring this level of precision (we must be among a special group of people who can talk about what's ordinary in surgeries of this sort), the surgeon will use a 3D CT scan to guide the drilling equipment. This scan is a backup protection that—in layman's terms—prevents the drill from going where it shouldn't, like into someone's *skull*. Turns out that equipment failed as the procedure was beginning. Anywhere else, they would have aborted the surgery, but this doctor decided to carry on without it—I guess he thought Jesus would take care of that small detail. Two days after, while Nathaniel was still in intensive care, the doctor left for Israel on a mission. We never saw him again, and we never sued him. We wanted the whole experience left in the past.

Thankfully, aside from future precautions, Nathaniel was fine. But damage radiates in ways that cannot be quantified. Up until then, my pregnancy had been going smoothly. I was still mowing the lawn, cleaning the house, playing with Nathaniel, eating healthily, and getting plenty of sleep. After the surgery, my energy changed. For the next month, I constantly hovered near Nathaniel to see if there was leakage. I was always nervous, always on edge. I will always believe that the trauma of that moment, the slip of the doctor's tool, had an effect on me that would reveal itself only after Jacob was born.

# 12. bad luck

Jacob's birth was normal, even exceptional in that I was one of those annoying people who experiences painless childbirth. (I'd paid my dues, right?) Also, Jacob came very fast — Russel raced on the shoulder of the highway, police cars chasing us, trying to make it before the baby arrived. When we pulled up to the hospital, two cops came toward us with guns drawn, ready to reclaim whatever we'd stolen, but one glance at my heaving body told them why we'd been speeding. A short twenty minutes later, Jacob was born.

Things had gone so smoothly that I only spent one night in the hospital, which was convenient. Nathaniel was staying with a neighbor while Russel's parents made their way from Hendersonville, a city nearly two hours away, near the mountains, and nobody but me had ever taken care of Nathaniel for long. (What if something happened, who would put the trach back in?) Jacob, only hours old, was already accommodating his brother.

There he was, ten fingers, ten toes, with his own quirks and delights and needs. Looking at the round, pink baby sleeping next to me in the hospital bed, I thought, *Oh my God, this is so easy, so comfortable, so peaceful.* I felt powerful, like I had accomplished something. Doctors and nurses stopped by and congratulated me, saying, "Look at him, he looks like a doll." So *this* was what most people experienced after childbirth: joy, pride, celebration. The horror movie audience was gone, and in their place the cooing smiles of a heartwarming family flick. I wondered if there was a way to find that experience even when your child had serious, unexpected complications.

The next day I was home, breastfeeding, and I said to Russel, "We are complete."

• • •

We didn't circumcise Nathaniel at birth because we were hoping to have a bris, but when he was a few months old, Dr. Ginsburg said prayers and performed the circumcision when Nathaniel was under anesthesia for another procedure. Since he had never had a ceremonial bris, we arranged for him to have his on the same day as his newborn brother's. We invited family and a few neighbors, including my friend Samantha. Russel's father brought some of his own friends, all of whom were liberals, and when they started talking politics with our Carolinian guests, the volume in the house escalated. Then Nathaniel had a meltdown, probably because he was jealous of the attention the baby was receiving, and as I was trying to calm him down, Samantha came up to me. Crying.

She said, "I feel so terrible for you."

I thought she was referring to Nathaniel's tantrum, but she continued. "It's just so sad that your children and my children won't be able to play together in heaven."

At first I was so distracted by Nathaniel's howling that I didn't get it. "Our children won't . . . what? What are you talking about?"

She explained, "Jewish people don't go to heaven."

Putting aside the ridiculousness of her assumption that our children would *still be children playing together* when they went to heaven, I could not believe how rude she was being. Thankfully, before I could kick her out of my house, Russel's father brought up politics, which led to him leaving in a huff. The party was over. And that was the last time I spoke to Samantha.

Soon after we brought Jacob home, Nathaniel, who was two and a half, started getting jealous. He was used to having me all to himself. He said, "It's time for that baby to go back to the hospital," and every so often would try to take a swipe at Jacob's head with one of his trains.

To ease the fratricidal tendencies, I tried to keep the routines that were familiar to Nathaniel. We still went to the park first thing every morning, before it got too hot. Jacob would nap in the stroller while I pushed Nathaniel on the swings.

At dinnertime, the four of us sat around the table, Nathaniel now in a regular chair and Jacob using the high chair in which Nathaniel had played with more food than he'd consumed. It was what families do all the time without even thinking: eating dinner together, squabbling, being told to take one more bite of broccoli, clamoring for dessert. It was what I'd grown up with in Poland without ever stopping to appreciate it, what I'd always expected to be my own family's life.

Afterward, we'd turn on the TV above the fireplace, switch the channel to Baby Looney Tunes, and all dance together, with me bouncing Jacob in my arms.

This was starting to feel like normal. It was all I had wanted.

But fate had a trick to play on me. Within a week of giving birth, I dropped to a size 0. The glands behind my ears swelled up. They looked like eggs. I went to the family doctor, who told me I was anemic.

A week or two later I felt like I was having a panic attack. I couldn't breathe. I went to the emergency room where they did an EKG to see if I was having a heart attack. It was stress, they told me. Maybe postpartum depression.

I had a pain in the middle of my spine—it made me walk funny—but I was too busy to pay much attention. We had decided to build a new house from the ground up, Russel was traveling a lot, and I had a toddler and a newborn.

My mother came to visit and found me weighing ninety pounds. (Have I mentioned that I'm 5'7"?) She took one look at me and asked, "What's wrong with you? Your skin is the color of dirt. Something's wrong." Every doctor I went to told me I had postpartum depression, and I believed them. Nathaniel's birth had been such a circus—maybe I'd reacted this way last time and hadn't noticed.

Our house in Charlotte sold more quickly than we thought it would, and the new house was far from being finished. For the first few months of Jacob's life, we stayed at the one-bedroom apartment of Russel's friend Oliver while he decamped to his girl-friend's place. A few times a week, Oliver and his girlfriend would come over and I'd cook them dinner as a small thank-you for a big kindness.

When the back pain got worse, Oliver took me for an MRI.

"There's nothing here," the doctors told me. "This is left over from the pregnancy. You need physical therapy." Again they suggested that it might be postpartum depression. They gave me OxyContin for the pain and Xanax for the stress.

I was so drugged up and miserable that when we moved to the new house, it barely registered. All I remember is that I didn't trust the mortgage guy when he told us that we'd been approved to buy the property. In Poland back then, at least in my village, there was no such thing as a mortgage. If you could afford a house, you bought it; otherwise, you kept saving. I didn't want us to live paycheck to paycheck, but everyone assured me that this was how it worked, especially in our new neighborhood. The banks were handing out mortgages like lollipops.

• • •

I was feeling worse and worse. By the time Jacob was four months old, I couldn't get warm. My whole jaw hurt from my teeth chattering.

My father came to visit. At one point he was downstairs, and I was up in my bedroom, shaking so much that I was having weird little convulsions. It was hard to utter a word through my shivers. I managed to moan "Dad" loudly enough for him to hear me.

He came into the room and asked, "What's the matter?"

I had three blankets piled on the bed and asked him for a fourth.

"Magda, something is seriously wrong with you. I think you're really sick," he said. "What kind of doctor did you go to?" Then he went down the road that any parent of an immigrant has traveled: "Why did you come to this country? Look what is happening to you. You should come back to Poland with me."

A week after my dad left, I could no longer walk up the stairs. I'd crawl up on all fours and slide back down on my butt, sometimes with the baby snug under one arm. I sat on the floor to prepare meals, peeling potatoes as I leaned against the cabinet, bowl between my legs, like a rag-doll Cinderella. To an outsider it probably looked like I was practicing a new parenting philosophy: Be on their level! Model crawling! It's not a hard doctrine to follow if standing up to change a diaper causes you excruciating pain.

Russel was at the end of his rope. The doctors had told him I was depressed and he had sympathy for that, but my physical suffering seemed over the top. He worked all day and came home to a household that was holding on by a thread. The strain began to show. One night I was up in my room shivering and I overheard him on the phone downstairs.

"Magda is really faking it. All the doctors say she's depressed.

I've been dealing with this for four months. She says she can't breathe, she can't walk, she's got pain. I don't know what I'm going to do with her. She doesn't want to be a mother."

I thought, *I'm dying. I'm literally dying.* I crawled down the hall to the top of the stairs and spoke to Russel through the spindles of the banister. "Look at me—I'm not making this up. I've never had pain like this. My body is failing me; I'm dying. You want me to die. I want a divorce. If you don't take me to a doctor tomorrow morning, I'm going back to Poland where my family who loves me will save my life." Then I went to sleep.

Russel made an appointment with a doctor for the next morning. He shook me awake at 7:00 a.m., saying "get out of bed" in a mean voice, like I was lazy. He was really frustrated with my ongoing complaints. I drove myself to the doctor. On the way there I threw up, all over myself and the car, green as if I'd been eating spinach. When I pulled up to the emergency entrance of the hospital, a volunteer was standing outside, helping direct people.

"Can I please have a wheelchair?" I asked. I was crying and covered with vomit. He followed me to a parking spot and helped me into a wheelchair. I rolled myself to the building. When I got to the doctor's office, I lay down on the examining table to wait. They brought me warm blankets, and I dozed off until he showed up.

"Hi, Mrs. Newman, what brings you in?" He had a cheerful, almost feminine voice. I could barely talk. He felt my lymph nodes. Suddenly his face was serious. "I see that you're underweight. Let's X-ray your lungs."

They brought an X-ray machine into the room. Ten minutes later the doctor came back with paperwork. He said, "Well, Mrs. Newman, first we have to do some blood work to rule out blood cancers, but even without looking at that, I feel certain that you have cancer, and it's pretty far advanced. I'm not an oncologist, just a family doctor, but I want to show you something."

He pointed at the X ray. "Your lungs are three-quarters full of fluid. That's because your lymph nodes are so swollen. You have shivers, high fever, weight loss, and bad pain. These are signs of leukemia or lymphoma."

Crying hysterically, I grabbed his shoulders and said, "Thank you."

I called Russel to tell him they were doing bloodwork to confirm cancer. He came straight to the doctor's office, got down on his knees in front of me and the doctor, and begged me to forgive him. "I failed you. I never deserved you in the first place, and I failed you."

Three years earlier, Russel had gotten a stable job so I would agree to move to the United States and marry him. That summer, I returned to the Hamptons to babysit for the same family I had worked for the year before. Russel spent the week in the city, then joined me on the weekends to wait tables and bartend at the same restaurant, which was now run by the Argentinian celebrity chef Francis Mallmann and called Patagonia West. Patagonia West was the "it" restaurant of the summer, and Russel was serving celebrities like the cast of the *Sopranos*, earning more in a weekend of bartending than he did at his office job all week.

One night, the mayor of Westhampton Beach came into the bar. After he'd had a few drinks, Russel persuaded him to officiate our wedding and to let us have the ceremony in a Westhampton park for free. As a lawyer, Russel insisted that he get their agreement in writing. And, like every agreement ever made in a bar, this one was scrawled on a napkin.

A couple days later, Russel showed up at town hall and showed his napkin to the secretary. She was incredulous, but the mayor had signed it so they had to honor it.

On September 8, 2002, we were married in a little gazebo in the center of Westhampton village. About thirty-five people came, and the mayor officiated, as promised. Afterward, Francis Mallmann had a reception for us at his restaurant. The waitstaff, who were Russel's friends, worked for free. This entire fantastic event probably cost him a grand total of $700 (after all, he did need to rent a tuxedo). As for me, I went to the East Village and on a rack outside a boutique found a white dress that went down to my ankles for $75. It was perfect for getting married in a beach town. I had left a prestigious music school behind, but the way he pulled together the wedding highlighted what I loved about Russel. He was clever, resourceful, and determined. He kept trying to prove himself to me, but I never doubted that I had made the right decision.

That fall we rented an apartment on the Upper East Side of Manhattan and started our life together. It was love and marriage in a 400-square-foot three-story walkup. The single window looked out on a brick wall that was four inches away. We loved it.

Now I was so sick that I didn't dwell on Russel's mistake. I understood it. I had gone to so many doctors, and all of them diagnosed my symptoms as postpartum or psychological. I was either faking or suffering from a mental breakdown. The doctors were so convincing that I myself had started to believe them. When we talk about it now, Russel doesn't make excuses, but I remind him of our timeline: We met in the summer of 2001 and married in the summer of 2002. Less than a year later, I was pregnant. Nathaniel was born in February of 2004. It all happened very quickly. If we'd been together longer, he would have known that I was tough and rarely complained, and that shirking my role as a mother was antithetical to my very core. Even so, maybe it was too much for him to imagine that we could have another stroke of bad luck. Probably he was just too tired to think straight. Also, it is just impossible to understand, under any circumstances, the toll that a highly needy baby takes on a person. If my pain turned inward, Russel's turned outward. There was nothing to forgive.

It took a few hours in the hospital basement to do a PET scan and bone marrow biopsy, then I went home to wait for the results.

I was standing in the bathroom of the new house when the doctor who would be my oncologist called. His name, coincidentally, was Dr. Newman, and he was young. I could tell from his voice he did not have good news.

"It's Hodgkin's lymphoma," he said, then paused.

"Okay," was my response. I had already suspected that would be the diagnosis.

Then he said, "It's stage IV. This means it's spread widely through your body. You have tumors in every organ and in your bone marrow."

I had a four-month old baby, a three-year-old with Treacher Collins, and stage IV Hodgkin's lymphoma. A tumor had fractured my spine, which explained why walking was so painful. Another tumor, as big as two fists, was pushing on my heart, which was why I had thought I was having a heart attack.

I wanted a second opinion, but the oncologist told me, "You don't have time for second opinions. This is stage IV. Thirty percent of your bone marrow is cancerous. Every hour counts; we have to begin treatment tomorrow."

I stood there holding the phone, tears coming down my cheeks, and started to hyperventilate. "Am I going to die?"

The doctor was quiet for a moment, then said, "It's a possibility. If we leave it untreated, you will die."

I pressed him for more information. "How much longer will I live without chemo?"

He said, "Two months, maximum. You're going to have a very rough course of chemo. It will either kill you or cure you."

That afternoon and the next morning, I stayed in my bedroom. Russel's parents came over to help out with Nathaniel and Jacob, but nobody ventured into my room to reassure me. Nobody told me I might be okay. Who knew what to do or say? I was a dying woman.

I didn't see the boys. I didn't eat anything. I just screamed and cried. *Why, why, why was I even born? Who would take care of my kids? Who would sacrifice their life to take care of Nathaniel?* I was already drugged up on painkillers and Xanax for my anxiety, and now I was scared that I was dying and angry that nobody had believed me. I was so desperate and broken in my body and soul that I couldn't stop screaming. It actually kind of helped me feel better.

My parents were devastated to hear the news. In Poland, when you hear the word *cancer* it's the end of the world. When my grandfather had cancer, I had no idea. He was sick, but nobody talked about his diagnosis. Then I found a bottle of pills or syrup stowed away on top of the refrigerator. I'd seen a commercial on TV for this particular medication, advertising it as "a miracle cure for cancer."

"Does Grandpa have cancer?" I asked my mother.

"No, no," she said. "We're just trying all the options."

My mother was so strong when I called her in a panic after

having given birth to Nathaniel, but she was hopeless when I had lymphoma. I truly think that they didn't believe my diagnosis. I was too young for this. Deep down, in their hearts, they thought it had to be a different disease. That's what got them through. Maybe they'd thought the same thing about my grandfather.

When Nathaniel was born, I couldn't understand why God had done this to him or had given him to me. Later I felt like I was chosen, like God picked me to raise this child. I was resolved to make something good from him being born with Treacher Collins. Now I questioned God again, this time with more anger and doubt. I asked, *Where are you? Are you kidding me? I gave up my life for this kid. I do everything for him. Now you're going to take my life away? Why are you punishing me again?*


How could I get cancer? Russel grew up in a place where everyone ate processed foods. They lived under power lines. They parked in underground garages, microwaved plastic, and used talcum powder. They sprayed pesticides in their homes and cleaned them away with chemicals. They were subject to every known or suspected cancer risk in the modern world.

When you have cancer, or a child with a genetic mutation for that matter, you can't help asking yourself if it's your fault, somehow connected to something you did. But I couldn't find any way to blame my upbringing. I grew up on an organic farm in Eastern Europe with no packaged foods, no hormones, no chemicals. When I came to the United States I'd never even taken an antibiotic. When I was a kid, I knew restaurants existed, but my mom always warned, "You never know what's in that food. You are what you put in your body."

We ate the vegetables and fruit that we grew on the farm. Like all children of farmers, my siblings and I had daily chores. We each had parts of the garden we were responsible for weeding. No fourteen-year-old kid wants to weed a cabbage patch, but we had no choice—if we wanted to eat, we had to help raise the food. We also went fishing and ate what we caught. The greatest fun of all was mushroom picking.

Mushroom season lasts for only a couple months at the end of summer. My father would wake three of us—the oldest of the six kids who would eventually form our family—at three in the morning. (My mother never came with us. Someone had to stay home to sell tomatoes and make sure people didn't jump the fence to steal food from the farm. Once she stopped a thief who tried to steal all our shoes—she beat him with a broom and called the police.)

With little backpacks that my mom packed full of lunch and snacks and carrying cute woven baskets, we drove to the woods. By the time we got there, it was dawn. We watched the sun rise and headed straight into the wilderness. There were no trails, but my father had a great sense of direction. No matter how far we wandered, he could always find his way out. He knew where and how to find mushrooms, even when we hadn't been there for a while. He showed us which mushrooms were poisonous and which were considered to be the top of the mushroom royal family. Cheap mushrooms grew on top of tree stumps, but the higher quality ones knew better—they hid in the moss. Mushrooms that were spongy under the cap were tastier than those with slits. The very best was the *prawdziwek*, which means "the real mushroom."

We would race through the woods, competing for the best haul. It was always an adventure. The first time Michal joined us, he stood up from searching around a shady stump and said, "What's that? Something's hitting my foot!" It was a snake, striking his boot again and again. He was so little he had no idea what it was.

We'd get home a few hours later, clean the mushrooms, cut them up, and spread them out to air-dry. Some went into jars of sauce that we would use for dinner. Others were reserved for soup. My mother kept some dried mushrooms in a special cotton sack for use throughout the year, and the rest were pickled.

The work we put into collecting mushrooms gave the food we ate deeper meaning. I love cooking with mushrooms, but the farmed ones sold at the grocery store don't compare to the ones I grew up eating. My family ships me dried mushrooms in Ziploc bags, and whenever someone visits from Poland, they sneak some through customs. Using them in my recipes makes my house smell as good as when my mother cooked them, bringing back happy memories of the woods, my childhood, my family.

Growing up on an organic farm also meant that my father never, ever used chemicals on his crops. His vigilance in this was absolute, and it led to what was, at the time, one of the most horrifying evenings of my life.

One year we had a plague of huge black slugs. They were six inches long, looked like small snakes, and left trails of slime on the tomato plants, ruining them. Of course my father wouldn't use pesticide, so he began sitting guard in the greenhouse, watching the slugs until he understood their behavior patterns. After a few days of this, he told us that, based on his observations, the slugs would come out when the sun went down, party on the tomatoes for a while, then go back into the ground. There was only one way to get rid of them: Pick them off by hand. That was where we kids came into the picture.

Our slug removal efforts began late at night, around 10:00 p.m. My father gave each of us a plastic bag and a flashlight, and assigned us each rows of tomato plants that were so thickly covered in slugs, all you could see was black. Cringing, I made my way down my rows, picking off all the nasty slugs by hand and depositing them in the plastic bag. I must have collected at least a hundred. At school, my classmates already teased me for being a farm girl; they called me "carrot." I was furious and embarrassed by this new indignity. Nobody else had to do things like this.

When we had purged our designated rows of slugs, we delivered our bags to my father and he threw them onto a campfire. They made a hissing sound as they burnt and we all screamed. This collection and slaughter went on for a few nights until there were no slugs left to be found. That's how crazy my dad was about not putting chemicals on crops.

As we get older, we realize that the best memories aren't just the happiest ones but the ones that stick. Now, twenty-five years later, those black slugs are still sliming their way around my head. No doubt they will be there forever, and I treasure the permanence of that moment, singular enough to stand out among the gathered days of my childhood. Not a bad realization for the mother of a kid whose early days were full of surgeries. I hoped that the hospital visits would blend together into a routine, forgettable blur, but also that if bad moments stood out, one day the pain (or sliminess) of them would recede, leaving only a proud war story.

Russel finds it ironic and infuriating that my wholesome childhood didn't guarantee me a cancer-free life. No doctor can say what caused my cancer—like many cancers it begins when a cell mutates—but in my heart of hearts I had a completely unscientific explanation for how it had happened. I remain convinced that the cancer was triggered six months earlier, when Nathaniel's surgery went wrong. The moment the doctor came out of the OR and told us he had accidently poked Nathaniel's brain didn't fall into the "oopsy daisy, we all make mistakes" category. It was easy to see the shock and stress of that moment compromising my immune system and opening the door to cancer.

The chemo was like a miracle. After the very first treatment, my pain was gone. I came home and said, "If this is what chemo does, I want more!" Even Dr. Newman was surprised that the improvement was so quick. When I showed up for my second treatment, I was already standing up straight again.

I was supposed to have chemo every other week for six months, for a total of twelve rounds, but halfway through the medications started to hit me and one of my lungs collapsed. They had to slow down the frequency of my treatments, so the whole process ended up taking eight months.

One night, after the chemo had started taking its toll, Russel saw Nathaniel walk into our room, where I was sleeping. He had just become a big brother, and his mother hadn't been the same since. As Russel watched, he stuck out his little hand and appeared to sprinkle something on my head.

"What are you doing to Mommy?" Russel asked.

"I'm sprinkling magic dust on her so she gets better," Nathaniel said.

Russel cried when Nathaniel said this, and he cried when he told it to me, and he cries every time he tells that story. He says, "However flawed I was, I was raising a little boy who, for all his own challenges, was determined to help and heal his mother."

## 13. casseroles and pity

I was physically ill, and I lamented the loss of the life I'd expected to have and the support I'd planned to give my sons. Sometimes, alone in the bathroom, I would scream. Russel always knew when to keep the kids away so they didn't see their mother at her weakest.

Meanwhile, our neighbors were appearing on our doorstep, bringing casseroles and pity. They said, "Bless you hard," encouraging me to read the Bible and prepare to hug Jesus. My neighbor Karen, a truly kind woman, had her whole church praying for me. It felt like they were praying for my soul since they already considered me a lost cause.

I thanked them politely but what I wanted to say was, *Would you be excited to meet Jesus if you were in my shoes?* It reminded me of how people had behaved in the hospital when Nathaniel was born. Nobody said congratulations because they were already grieving.

One time I invited Donna, a friend I'd made in the chemo room, over for lunch with her husband. Russel took him out back to show him the houses that were under construction in our development. They were nearly finished, but unfurnished and never locked. Sometimes, we'd walk over with the kids and make up stories about the dragons that lived there, but adults liked to snoop around too, checking out floorplans and guessing what they would sell for.

When the men disappeared, Donna confided, "Magda, I can't say this in front of my husband. Everyone tells me I'm blessed, that Jesus is waiting for me, but I'm not ready; I don't want to die. I'm mad at God. I have young kids and I want to see them grow up. I don't feel religious anymore. I'm so scared."

When I went to chemo three days later, her chair was empty. She'd only been in her forties, and she had lost her battle.

Like Donna, I wasn't so devout that I could come to terms with death. I wanted to live.

Support came from the most unexpected places — angels we never looked for appeared as if sent. A cousin of mine who lived in Chicago put me in touch with Kalina, a Polish friend of his. It literally was like: "Oh, you have cancer? My friend had cancer. You guys have so much in common!"

In the beginning, when I was digesting the fact that I was sick, Kalina called me every night. She'd had cancer twice and had been in remission for ten years. She knew how to give me strength, and her confidence that I would survive made me start thinking that maybe I would actually make it. Over the phone, this woman I had never met told me, "You have nothing to worry about. I am psychic. I know you're going to be fine, just like I am."

Kalina believed in tough love and was not one to mince words. If I said I was afraid I wouldn't survive, she'd say something like, "You're going to give up and let some bitch raise your kids? I thought you were better than that! Don't sit around pitying yourself. This is just a bump in the road." Someone else might have found her too harsh, but she made me laugh. It was exactly what I needed.

Russel had no idea how to comfort me. All he did was cry. When I cried, he cried. But he instantly recognized what Kalina did for me. The minute she'd call Russel would spring to action: "Okay, everybody, come with me. Mom's talking to Kalina." He'd gather the kids and vanish.

Kalina was my guru. She had survived, so I did whatever she told me to do. If she said beet juice was good for my blood, I drank beet juice. If she told me to be selfish and sleep when I was tired, I obeyed. My attitude started to shift from victim to survivor.

People had warned me that losing my hair would be traumatic. Following their advice, I went to a wig-maker in Charlotte. She studied my face and coloring and made me an expensive wig from real hair. It was a brown bob and I looked like an old lady in it, which, come to think of it, was not a bad match for how I felt. I had the wig on hand, but when I went to a salon to get my head shaved, they told me not to do it all at once because it would be easier to accept if I started with a bob and then got a pixie cut, and waited to shave it until it fell out. Oh, and did it fall out! I was taking a shower after my third round of chemo and when I looked down, I saw that the whole floor of the stall was covered with hair. I reached up to my head and—hair fell into my hands. It was clogging the drain. I went into the shower with hair and came out nearly bald. It would have been much less traumatic to shave it sooner. The next day I went to a salon and asked the stylist to take the rest off.

Kalina's "think positive" attitude was in the air. One Friday night a week or so after I lost my hair, two of Russel's frat brothers showed up with a plan. As we joked around over pizza, the guys declared their intention to shave their heads in solidarity with me. They took a chair and a bowl of water out onto the patio and then, with beers in their hands and music playing, Russel and his friends took turns shaving one another's heads. Afterward, we took pictures of us all standing together, a bald quartet. When they left the next day, one of them handed me *The Secret* by Rhonda Byrne, which was on the bestseller list at the time, and said, "I feel like you should read this book."

People often turn to religion and self-help books when dealing with illness or medical challenges. The dominant message of the Christian books that I'd been given was that we should accept Nathaniel as he was born, or that I should joyfully accept the fact that I was dying and that I was lucky because I would soon be in heaven with Jesus.

I swallowed *The Secret* whole. The book preached a shift in thinking, and it inspired me to take control of my destiny. I saw that I had two choices: to stay angry, live in a dark world, and have my kids see and grow up with that, or to find a way to focus on positive things. Talking to Kalina and reading *The Secret* set me on a new path. I chose to embrace life, to fight for myself and for the best life I could give Nathaniel.

I worked hard at not being upset. Instead of spiraling about cancer, I envisioned the outcome I wanted. I made a point of telling myself that I would be okay, that I had the kids to live for. From then on, whenever I heard someone had cancer, the first thing I did was give them that book. It may be a voodoo philosophy, but the underlying message for me was that God exists. Because what is thinking positive if it not having faith? And who is the person who tells you to believe this if not a messenger from God?

There were angels in our life who showed their hearts when we had moments of despair. When Nathaniel was born, Russel's bosses let him work from home. One day they handed him a $6,000 check. The company had passed a hat to help us pay for frozen ready-made meals and a cleaning service. We didn't have to search for these angels. They were already among us.

Some people try to stand out. Maybe they draw attention to themselves by looking different — by getting tattoos or wearing bright clothes or dyeing their hair purple. But Nathaniel was noticed from the moment he was born and from then on, without asking for attention or saying a word. He wasn't given the choice. I, as his mother, received similar attention, which always fell under the category of "What's wrong with you? What's wrong with your child?" When I was a competitive pianist, I liked the attention I received being on stage; it energized me. But this was different.

Beauty is an accident just as much as Treacher Collins is an accident, but either way, your appearance shapes you by shaping how people react to you. When Russel first noticed me, I was walking around Southampton wearing a big floppy hat and black bathing suit, having my Audrey Hepburn moment. I enjoyed being looked at, being a young girl and feeling pretty. Seeing how people responded to Nathaniel changed my relationship with beauty. People put so much stock in it, and here I was with a child who would never fit into the norms. I stopped seeing beauty as an external quality. Beauty, to me, became the people who reacted to my baby with care, love, hope, and joy.

One way I found to think positive was to wear my hot, uncomfortable, ugly wig most of the time. It was summer in North Carolina, but I never went outside without it, hiding my baldness not because I wanted to look beautiful, but so I wouldn't have to see people's reactions to me. It wasn't a matter of vanity; I didn't want to have to explain that I had cancer because I didn't want their pity. I had never wanted it for Nathaniel and I didn't want it for myself. I hate pity.

I'd deliberately shifted from having one foot in the coffin to convincing myself I was indestructible. No longer would I let myself entertain the possibility of failure. I didn't think it through at the time, but somewhere was the instinct that if I looked perfectly healthy and everyone saw me that way, it would keep me in that frame of mind.

*Nathaniel: I don't overthink my appearance. When I wake up I don't stare at the mirror. I just feel like myself. I don't even notice my scars unless I'm focusing on them. I see what I want to see. And when it comes to Treacher Collins, I find the positive. I can do things other kids can't do. I can turn off my hearing aid when my brother is being annoying, and because my BAHA has Bluetooth, I can listen to music without headphones. That's right—I can play music in my head. Pretty bionic.*

*And for some reason, one feature of Treacher Collins is that I have extra hair on my body, including my face. My mom asked if I wanted to shave the sideburns on my cheeks, but I like them. I'm not trying to look like everyone else. I'd rather look like Wolverine. Also, considering I have a fairly severe case of Treacher Collins, I say I'm pretty hot.*

On doctor's orders, I avoided public places while I was undergoing chemo. My immune system was vulnerable. My mouth had blisters and my gums were bleeding. My teeth turned yellow and felt loose. I looked like a heroin addict.

The only way I know I tried to be a good mother during that time is because in our photo albums there are pictures of the kids painting the wooden fence in the backyard, and I know that means I still tried to give them fun things to do. But what I remember most was being tired. All the time. Nathaniel was always content to play with his trains, but Jacob, being only six months old, demanded more attention, so I napped when he napped. Sometimes I would pull out every toy in the house, lie down on the floor, and rest while they played by themselves. Jacob, who needed more cuddling than Nathaniel ever had, would crawl on top of me while I slept.

I was taking care of two small children, trying to cook and give them baths and make sure they were entertained. I did my best, but it was a difficult time. When I look back on photos of myself from that time, I see a woman drugged up on painkillers, trying to come back from the dead. I remember driving in my car with the boys, Jacob screaming in his car seat because he was in that phase where he hated being restrained by the seatbelt. When talking to him calmly failed, and singing my favorite silly Polish song about a cucumber failed, sometimes I found myself screaming along with him.

Ultimately, the message that I found in my illness was that God was telling me to slow down and take care of myself. I stopped bemoaning my fate and started living. I went outside for fresh air. I bought a juicer and started paying closer attention to what I ate. I tried to send out positive energy and to surround myself with it. For me, forgiving was part of that. I was still plagued by the same envy that I had felt when Nathaniel was born. I saw women who had jobs and vacations, with gym memberships and pretty clothes and healthy, "normal" children who could frolic in the pool all day long. If I held on to that envy, I would never be a happy person. I had a second chance to live and it was up to me to be happy or sad, to enjoy the sunshine or see a cloud on the horizon.

The night after Donna didn't show up for chemo, I lay in bed and made God a promise. *I know you're there. I know you're listening. If you let me live, I can't promise I'll go to church every Sunday. I don't even know what religion you prefer.* (I'd seen many different religions in the chemo room and still couldn't find a reason that one idea of God was better than another.) *But I promise you that if I live, I'll give back. I'll do good. I'll be a good person and I won't expect anything in return. I'll do something good every day.*

When I was first diagnosed with cancer, the doctor had told me how serious my condition was. But he also pointed out that I was young and my body was strong, which worked in my favor. The chemo hadn't killed me, so it had cured me. The day of my final treatment, the nurses in the chemo room gave me a diploma to celebrate my graduation. I gave each of them an infinity necklace studded with cubic zirconia. I liked the infinity sign and what it suggested about the circle of life. I wrote each of them a note thanking them for helping me.

I survived, I believe God wanted me to live, and I give thanks for that. This is obviously a problematic way of thinking. I didn't believe that God wanted Donna to die, but it was useless to over-think it. I was in survival mode. I needed a way to cope, and I found strength in the combination of my voodoo psychology and my belief that God had a plan and that he heard me.

## 14. we've got this

Being a mom was almost taken away from me, and I had faced the realistic possibility that someone else might raise my kids because I wasn't around. I'd been under the surface, almost at the bottom, without knowing if I'd ever come up. As I made my way back to sunlight, I clearly saw what was most important to me. I was so grateful to have more time with my children, and I wanted to give them a happy life. Cancer inspired me to be a better mother.

With a newborn baby, Nathaniel's medical encumbrances, and my illness, the boys and I hadn't ventured far from the house for the first year of Jacob's life. But gradually I felt stronger and started planning outings for us. We weren't exactly foraging for mushrooms, but we spent lots of time at the local discovery museum. There was a big pile of dirt where they could dig, and water tables where they could pretend to pan for gold. When the boys lost themselves in exploration, or as I collected books and stickers on a topic like butterflies or spiders, those were the times when I felt like the mother I had always wanted to be, replicating a version of the happy childhood I remembered. And in spite of my constant anxiety, I refused to treat Nathaniel as sickly or fragile. I didn't want that to be part of his identity.

Then I found a dream trip for the boys. There was a Thomas the Tank Engine–themed week at Tweetsie Railroad, an amusement park about two hours outside Charlotte. We would ride a life-sized Thomas through the Blue Ridge mountains, there would be storytelling, and afterward, if we were up to it, we could try out classic rides like a carousel and a Ferris wheel.

The Day Out With Thomas was the most ambitious outing our family had ever made. It was a long-awaited treat for us — Nathaniel, three years old, had recovered from his most recent surgery, and one-year-old Jacob was just getting big enough to enjoy such excursions. I was done with chemo and starting to feel stronger, but still wearing a wig.

The first thing that went wrong was that Jacob decided to hurl his pacifier out the train window — then immediately regretted that move. Being a toddler is hard that way. Jacob expressed his regret by howling for the rest of the ride. This was a disaster, though not on the scale of the hearing aid falling into the toilet full of pee.

Every parent has been there: trying to calm one child while trying to ensure the other one gets to enjoy what was supposed to be a fun day. Then the train encountered a tree that had fallen across the tracks. We had to stop and return to the station going backwards. At the time, I assumed this was another hitch in our plans, but in hindsight it seems very possible that it was a planned part of the ride, meant to add drama to our experience. Not that we needed it—we were making plenty of drama all on our own.

It looked like our luck was changing (or so we thought). The gift shop at the end of the line had train-themed everything, and Russel miraculously found lollipops shaped like pacifiers. Soon Jacob was happily sucking and hopped up on sugar. So, toddler soothed at last, we started exploring the rest of the park.

We were contemplating our options when I noticed that the front of Nathaniel's shirt was wet. At first I thought he was sweating, but Russel and I soon realized that every sip of water he took was spilling out of his stomach. It was surreal—his g-tube had become dislodged. What we felt was a little like the panic you might feel if a pipe burst in your house and water spurted out, ruining everything, except what was leaking was our child, and there was no shut-off valve. He was in danger of infection and dehydration. Not a drop of fluid was staying in his belly.

We called Pat Chibbaro, our nurse friend from NYU. Having sworn off the ENT who nearly killed Nathaniel, the only doctor we had in Charlotte was a pediatrician. Pat knew we weren't eager to return to the hospital where we'd had such a bad experience. She had a friend who was a nurse practitioner in a children's hospital in Chapel Hill and told us it was the best place to go.

With a cloth diaper around Nathaniel's belly to soak up the fluids pouring out of him and Jacob loudly protesting being in the car seat, we sped from the Tweetsie Railroad to Chapel Hill, three hours away, where they replaced the g-tube. The procedure was horrendous but relatively fast. They had to rip it out, a sight that had made me faint in the past. The only upside was that they replaced it with a newer version that had to be changed more often, but was easier to put in.

Every mom has a story about a failed outing, right? The kid having a tantrum in the grocery store. The unappreciative toddler breaking down at the zoo. . . . I guess our day was kind of normal, if you substitute the stubbed toe with a dislodged g-tube.

Not long after the Thomas the Tank Engine debacle, we removed the g-tube for good. Nathaniel was getting enough food and gaining weight. I hadn't used it to feed him for a couple of years, but we had kept it as a security blanket, knowing that sometime in the future, he would probably need it for another jaw surgery. Eventually I came to believe that putting in another one later would be better than having him endure the discomfort and risk of playing with it in. He already had a hearing aid and a trach to worry about, and we wanted him to be more carefree. Russel and I talked to Dr. McCarthy and he agreed.

Removing the g-tube was a very quick surgery, but a huge day —one fewer hole in Nathaniel's body. Now he could go down the slide on his belly the way he wanted to, and he didn't have to worry about it catching on the edge of a table. He had been cautious about this foreign part of his body for all of his first four years—"Be careful! Watch your g-tube!"—when all he should have been thinking about was playing and avoiding skinned knees.

I, too, was freed. No more flushing the tube so it wouldn't get clogged. No more using silver nitrate on a stick to burn off the granulation tissue that would collect around it. No more medical procedures that were a foreign language to 99 percent of the world. We celebrated at Cheesecake Factory, Nathaniel's favorite restaurant at the time. I felt like the sky was smiling. We were one more step closer to "normal."

# 15. teaching and being taught

I survived cancer, and then the bills started rolling in. Even after insurance, we owed thousands of dollars here and there as we met various deductibles and paid for medical supplies that inexplicably wasn't covered (like the BAHA hearing aid). As always, we were expected to pay up front and wait for insurance to reimburse us. Between Nathaniel's most recent surgery, my cancer, and our big new mortgage, it was too much.

I kept telling Russel, "I'm stressed out. We have to sell the house and downsize."

One day he came home and said, "I have an opportunity to make more money, but we would have to move to Connecticut." From the start, I had been uncomfortable with the loan we'd taken out to build the house in Charlotte. I didn't think we could afford it, and once I got sick, it became clear that we couldn't. We didn't even have the money for a dining room set, and that empty room bothered me.

All around us, people were living in large houses that were partially furnished. I wanted to downsize to something we could handle, and I wanted Russel to make more money so we were prepared for any other unpleasant surprises. This new job came with a bigger salary; it was closer to Nathaniel's doctors in New York; and we'd be near good doctors if I got sick again. I had an oncologist at Hartford Hospital, and if something went wrong I knew the doctor I would see at Memorial Sloan Kettering. We agreed that he should accept the offer.

Russel moved up to Connecticut to start work, and a few weeks later he called from the corporate apartment he was staying in and announced, "I found the best house." The house, a little Colonial dollhouse, was in West Hartford, with a hill right above it with nicer, more spacious homes. Apparently, the row of small houses had been built for the people who served the wealthy residents above. It sounded good enough to me: It had a garden and was right in the center of town, walking distance from an elementary school. It was in a great area, and houses in the neighborhood were selling as soon as they came on the market. There was a bidding war, and Russel bought it without my even seeing it.

My husband had a good career and earned a decent salary. His colleagues at the same level lived in big, beautiful homes. The first time I invited his new boss and his wife over for lunch, they didn't say a word but I noticed a bit of discomfort in their eyes when they saw where we lived. It wasn't what they expected from someone with Russel's position. I wanted to be proud of my house too, but we still had medical bills to pay.

Whenever vacation time rolled around, our friends and acquaintances would tell us about the trips to Hawaii or Disneyland they were planning. They would ski in the winter and rent a beach house for the summer, all the flags of material success. We had none of that. Instead, we had doctors to visit, surgeries that had to happen when school wasn't in session, and, as always, more bills to pay. We may not have been wealthy, but we had fresh tomatoes from the garden that I could pick and feed my kids, and, to my great relief, there were no gigantic black slugs to contend with.

For the first year or two after cancer, my goal was simply to make it to the next day. If I'd ever cared about having a fancy house, I didn't now. It no longer mattered to me. If I couldn't be happy without a better car, a better house, better furniture and clothes, I would never be happy. I decided to be happy with what I had, and the greatest treasures I had were my children.

• • •

We knew that when Nathaniel started kindergarten, he would be a surprise to his classmates. In the middle of the summer before school started, Russel contacted the principal, Dr. Nancy De-Palma, and told her about Nathaniel. He sent photos of him and materials explaining Treacher Collins, and said we'd like to bring him in for a meeting. It was an upbeat, casual get-together. Russel took the lead, and we explained Nathaniel's medical needs.

Dr. DePalma, a petite Italian American woman, happened to be the best principal that ever walked this planet. She said hi to all the parents at the door. She went from class to class, listening to teachers and greeting every kid by name. Even before we knew how engaged she was, when we first met her, she made it clear that she was thrilled to have Nathaniel at the school.

Russel told her that he had an idea. He said, "What if we write a letter to the school community? It could explain why Nathaniel looks the way he does. Maybe it would help everyone start off on the right foot."

Dr. DePalma loved the idea, and when she read his draft, she said, "This is brilliant. I can't wait." Her praise felt surprisingly good—we were flying blind and hers was the first real affirmation that we weren't completely blowing this parenting thing.

Russel wrote the letter from Nathaniel's perspective. It began "Hi! My name is Nathaniel Newman. I am in your son's/daughter's class. I had a really great idea. You see, I figure by now your kid has maybe asked a few questions about me or talked about me when he/she came home from school today. Bet it would help if I told you a little more about myself." The letter explained Treacher Collins syndrome in such a way that if parents read it to their children, they would both have all their questions answered:

*TCS makes it so that when you're growing in Mommy's belly, the bones in your face forget to grow like the rest of your bones. What happened to me was a lot of my bones forgot to grow. AND I EVEN GREW SOME YOU'RE NOT SUPPOSED TO HAVE! They tell me that this sort of makes me a miracle! Cool, but a bit silly, because isn't every kid in our class a miracle? Here is some of the different stuff about me:*

*—I have no ears. But here is the amazing part: I hear everything you do! The stuff inside my head that makes you hear (eardrums, bones, nerves) are all there. Just no flippy floppy ears on the outside. This is called microtia. How do I hear, you ask? I have an amazing thing called a BAHA hearing aid. I call it my magic ear. It's a small brown thing that I wear on a colorful headband.*

*—I have no cheekbones and my eyes slant down because there aren't enough bones holding up my eyeballs! They say they can fix this when I'm older. I'm not in a rush because that means another trip to NYU Medical Center. I've had like twenty surgeries there. I think that's plenty for now!*

*—My jawbone is really, really small. So is the inside of my mouth. The shape of my mouth, palate, throat, and airway is all a bit different. As a baby it was hard for me to eat and breathe, but I figured it out and now I eat like all the other kids at school.*

*—One really serious thing I have to tell you about: Remember how I said I have some extra bones? Mine grew in a pretty yucky place: the back of my nose! I have a really cute nose on the outside, but on the inside there's a wall of solid bone at the back. This one has a hard name to say: complete bilateral choanal atresia. It does make some stuff real hard for*

*me, especially breathing. That's why they put a hole in my throat with a cool tube sticking out of it. It's called a tracheostomy. At school, I wear a nifty purple cap over it so I can still talk real loud, and it helps me keep dirt out.*

The letter may have been too long, but better to err on the side of too much information than not enough. We gave the parents suggestions for what they might tell their kids: not to stare and not to touch the trach or hearing aid. We also explained that because of his nose being blocked, sometimes it ran and he didn't notice it. If his nose was running, instead of laughing at him, the kids should just tell him to wipe it and he would.

Finally, we asked them to treat Nathaniel like everyone else. We told them Treacher Collins didn't impact his mental or emotional development. And we finished by saying they could call with questions.

The letter helped set up Nathaniel for an easy entry into kindergarten. If the parents communicated some or all of it to their kids, then everyone would know that someone who was different would be showing up, nobody would be caught off guard, the parents would have a chance to answer questions, and we could avoid some of the uncomfortable stares.

If you think about it, how many parents send their children off to school hoping their classmates will embrace their differences and welcome them? Most kids have doubts and insecurities, but Nathaniel's struggles were on display. What would it be like if everyone could write a letter to their future classmates saying, "Here are the unusual things about me. Please don't be scared. Ask me anything you want. I just want to make friends and play"?

On the first day of school, we went to Nathaniel's classroom and introduced him to his classmates. I sat in a circle with them on the floor and asked, "Do you want to know why Nathaniel looks like this? It's just the way he was born." Then I said the same thing I would say to curious children for years: "Touch your face. Feel your cheekbones. Nathaniel doesn't have cheekbones like you. That's why he looks different. That button on his neck helps him breathe. Please don't touch it. And the other button is his hearing aid." When I was done, I asked if they had any questions.

"I'm scared of him," one boy ventured.

"I'm sorry you feel that way," I said. "Why are you scared?"

"He looks scary," the boy elaborated.

I said, "He looks different, but different doesn't have to be scary."

Nathaniel didn't react much during this conversation. He waved hi when we sat down and smiled in a friendly way but, as always, didn't take a big interest in his own difference.

Later that year, Dr. DePalma said to me, "I know you're a good parent, even though I don't ever witness your parenting. I can tell by Nathaniel, his manners, how he interacts, how he listens and plays." No authority had ever told me that, and it meant a lot to me. There was no parenting book for my situation and I always felt like I was flying by the seat of my pants. It was nice to get a "good job!"—I hadn't even realized how much I'd needed it.

Dr. DePalma was brilliant and the school community was supportive, but outside of that, the beginning of elementary school was the worst point in Nathaniel's life when it came to being out in public. At the playground, in movie theaters, kids would point at him and say "Eeewwww." Some would cry and ask to leave. Parents were sometimes embarrassed, but we tried not to be sensitive to it. Just as I had with Jenna's daughter Emily, it's natural to have a reaction when someone looks dramatically different.

Also, children are naturally curious. As we get older, we learn to temper our reactions and be more sensitive to the feelings of the people around us. *Learn* is the key word here. If a kid looked at Nathaniel with fear, curiosity, or a mix, I spoke to them the same way I'd spoken to the children in his class: "This is Nathaniel. He's six years old. He was born this way. Do you want to know what's going on with his face? He has a syndrome called Treacher Collins . . ."

It wasn't my personal mission to explain Treacher Collins to all the children on all the playgrounds of the world, but I thought it was worthwhile to do a little grassroots campaigning. Discomfort is a natural human response—if I, his mother, experienced it when I first saw him, why shouldn't other people? My goal was to help parents and children move past that moment as quickly as possible and see Nathaniel for who he was, just like we did.

The best way for children to learn empathy is from their parents, and the ones we met would often take the time to show their kids there was no reason to be scared or stare, and they should just treat Nathaniel like a fellow child. But some parents were clueless. When Russel was in a good mood, he'd say to one of those parents, "This is a teachable moment. If your child says, 'Ooh, you look terrible. Were you in an accident or a fire?' you can gently guide them. It's okay to say, 'Do you mind if I ask you a question? What's on your neck?'"

But Russel grew up as a construction worker's kid with a self-diagnosed Napoleon complex. He was a hair-trigger fighter, and sometimes it was hard for him to hold back when a kid would say something like, "You're a freak!" or "You're a monster!"

If the mom or dad didn't get involved, Russel would go over and confront them. "You heard what your child said and you're just sitting there."

The parent sometimes responded, "What do you expect him to say? He's just a kid."

This happened two or three times every week, and it brought Russel to the edge. One time he came home and told me that he was about to sock some rude father, but he looked at Nathaniel and saw absolute fear in his eyes. He didn't like seeing his father so angry.

Russel continued, "All he wanted to do was play and have fun, and I was about to punch a middle-aged dad in the face because he was too stupid to teach his kid not to be rude. I thought, *Whoa, this is exactly what I don't want him to do when people treat him badly*, and I stopped myself." Now, he says proudly that by the grace of God and Nathaniel, he never had a physical alteration.

But occasionally, when Russel became frustrated by an older kid or adult who was staring, he'd pretend not to notice, then suddenly turn and bark right in their face like a dog. He called it a stare stopper. Weird, yes, but it definitely did the trick.

Jacob remembers being very small and seeing little kids stare wide-eyed at Nathaniel for up to two solid minutes. If they asked their parents what was on his neck, sometimes Jacob would answer. But if they started reaching for the trach, he would put his small body between them and defend Nathaniel until the nearest grownup took charge. When he got older, he liked to do the stare stopper with Russel.

In no small part because of Nathaniel's personality, the social issues we encountered never pierced the surface for us. We went wherever we wanted to go, and we sent Nathaniel into new situations without hesitation, not worrying about how strangers or new schoolmates might react. We handled rude reactions the way we would handle an annoyance like poison ivy: unpleasant, unwelcome, but easily soothed.

Nathaniel lives in his own world, where nothing is ever wrong. When he walks down the street, he only notices the good things. If someone is standing there cursing and someone else is walking a puppy, he only sees the puppy. He's accustomed to the stares and double takes when people first see him because he's gotten them his whole life—and if somebody says something mean like "his face is weird," he might give them a look, but keep walking, unbothered.

Jacob seems to be wired differently. If he'd had Treacher Collins, he's sure he would have had a panic attack before every surgery. Curious toddlers would have angered or saddened him, and he thinks that after a while he would've become so tired of it that he would verbally and physically attack people. He doesn't think he's as resilient as Nathaniel—when he's playing lacrosse, he loses his temper when things don't go his way. (It's something he's working on.) But we'll never know if Nathaniel was born equipped to deal with his challenges, or whether he rose to meet them because he had to.

*Nathaniel: My face was familiar to Jacob from the day he was born. He was the one person who had no idea that I was different until he saw people picking on me. He remembers that when he first heard people saying mean things, he looked at my face and couldn't see the difference. He'd been around people with craniofacial differences his whole life. Jacob grew up blind to "normal." But if you tell me I should feel grateful to have a little brother who always saw me for who I am, I will tell you that he's still a little brother, not an angel.*

The way children reacted to Nathaniel wasn't the only way his school experience was different from other kids. A nurse, paid for by the school district, had to be within a few feet of him at all times. The g-tube was gone, but he had a very expensive hearing aid that couldn't get wet or damaged, and the tracheostomy, which had to be suctioned if it got clogged or immediately replaced if it got dislodged. Unfortunately, the trach button was either red or purple, depending on which valve he was using, and because these colors were tempting, sometimes a kid on the playground would try to grab it. The nurse was there to intervene.

We lucked out. Lisa Nowak, the nurse supervisor for the school district, happened to be based at Nathaniel's school. She picked his nurses — one came three days a week, another the other two. Lisa wasn't warm and cuddly, but she was very organized and thorough: We had to provide numerous forms for her files, and if one was missing, she definitely wanted it. If anything happened to our son, it was reassuring to know that she was in the building.

Being Nathaniel's safety net was a full-time gig. In the summertime, when noses don't run, I'd only have to suction his trach maybe ten times a day. But if he was sick with a cold or a flu, or if it was humid, it could go up to seventy times. When he was sick, I would sleep next to him. In the middle of the night, half-asleep, I'd hear the raspy noise of mucus stuck in his throat. On autopilot, without getting out of bed, I would disinfect my hands, suction him, and fall back asleep.

At school, the nurse was the keeper of the suction, and she followed Nathaniel everywhere, including recess and the bathroom. Some nurses gave him more freedom than others, but they had to be strict when it came to the hearing aid. He could never wear it outside in the rain. He couldn't play sports and he had to be careful at recess.

He was only six, so he barely noticed that his experience was different. When you're that little, it's not that weird to have a grownup shadowing you; most kids are used to having a parent or a babysitter with them at all times until kindergarten starts. In Nathaniel's case, his personal caregiver just never went away. He also received other special services from his IEP (individualized education program). He had speech therapy for a few years; he took tests alone; and a psychologist monitored him to make sure he felt comfortable in school and was developmentally on track.

Nathaniel was legally deaf without his hearing aid (and legally blind in one eye, for that matter). I worried about him not hearing approaching cars—I had the city put "Deaf and Blind Child" signs on our street—but when he started school we realized something else. His hearing isn't directional. That means he hears all noise as if it's coming from the same place (no particular place) and the same distance (no particular distance). We knew this already. It drove him crazy in movie theaters because it was hard for him to separate the whispers of people in the audience (or popcorn-munching, or worse) from the voices on screen. But we'd never thought about how this difference would come into play at school.

If a teacher stood behind him and said, "Hey, Nathaniel, look at me. Can you hold your pencil just like this?" he would have no idea where the sound was coming from. It doesn't seem like a big deal, but being six years old in a kindergarten classroom is already chaotic and confusing enough. Not knowing where sounds were coming from dumped an extra dose of mayhem into the mix. After a couple of months, we solved the problem by finding him a different hearing aid that you could set to a specific channel. The teacher wore a special microphone that she could tune to that frequency, which elevated her voice above the background noise.

To be honest, the transition to school was harder for me than it was for Nathaniel. I was scared that he'd fall, tussle with another kid, or get caught in the rain. An everyday misstep could be life-threatening for him. I wasn't the only parent who had trouble leaving the classroom on their child's first day, but because Nathaniel was more fragile, the stakes for us were higher.

For the first month of school, I timed Jacob's walk in his stroller to Nathaniel's recess on the playground. This was my way of covertly making sure he was out there with the rest of them, having fun and still breathing. Eventually, I legitimized my spying by volunteering in his classroom and the school library, and teaching a yoga class to the students.

## 16. the new me

In Connecticut I came as close to building a dream life as was possible. Every mom knows that sending a kid off to kindergarten buys some measure of freedom. I had that, but supersized, given my new lease on life. Jacob and I walked Nathaniel to school every day. On the way back I'd stop at the Russian supermarket for Polish cold cuts. When we got home, I gave Jacob a snack, then it was naptime. Afterward, he might have a playdate.

The kids and I started a garden, planting strawberries, blueberries, tomatoes, and peppers. Jacob was more into this than Nathaniel. He loved to cook and clean and do household chores, whereas Nathaniel preferred to live in an imaginary world. I bought them cute watering cans, gardening gloves, and rakes. Nathaniel would pull the rake three times and call it a day. Jacob would water the tomato plants and check for tomatoes, then come in and say, "Mom, let's make something with these peppers."

We'd make a stew and at dinner I'd say, "Jacob grew these," and he'd beam with pride. If my second son was subconsciously looking for his own special connection with me, this was where he found it.

I bought myself a chainsaw and got rid of seven stumps in our yard. (Daughter of a farmer; it's in my blood.) Figuring the best way for the neighborhood kids to accept Nathaniel was to make our house the "fun" house, Russel and I salvaged an old rickety wooden swing-set. He power-washed and resurfaced it. I spread old sheets on the ground and laid out paint, brushes, sponges, and other tools for painting on them. Smocked in Russel's old shirts, the neighborhood kids went to town decorating the swing set, even painting the slide. After they left, I would repaint it brown, so they could do it all over again. I set out sprinklers for them to run under, and I took the boys and their little friends to the beach, which was only forty minutes away. We gathered seashells and stopped for ice cream in the afternoon. When we got home, I'd drill holes in the shells, then we'd have kids over for a shell-painting party, stringing them into wind chimes.

In walking distance from our house was beautiful Elizabeth Park, where we spent a good chunk of the weekends in spring and summer. We had picnics among the blooming tulips and roses, and listened to outdoor concerts.

Most everyone in West Hartford recognized our family because of Nathaniel. The first Christmas in that house, we didn't have much money, but we spent more than we could afford on a child's jeep. Very often we would walk to town, Nathaniel driving his jeep and Jacob in the stroller, to get ice cream, go to the movies, or stop by the library. Sometimes we would have Nathaniel's favorite mac 'n' cheese at a restaurant called the Elbow Room, where we would sit on the rooftop overlooking the Main Street of our cute New England town.

That first winter, the kids discovered snow and sledding. Jacob would go down a hill three times and come to me shivering and done, but Nathaniel would go until his lips were blue and I insisted we head home for dinner.

When I had cancer, I promised God that if I lived, I would do some good in the world. Being told I was dying at twenty-seven years old had made me like an old lady fighting death. From then on, I felt compassion for old people, forgotten like shadows. During chemo, whenever I felt well enough, I taught piano lessons to seniors at the Jewish Community Center.

Now I had the chance to give back in my new city. Instead of going to church, I wanted to find another way to do something kind. There was an assisted living facility near Jacob's preschool, so one day I walked in and told the person at the front desk I'd love to come volunteer once or twice a week.

They ran a background check on me and when they determined that I wasn't a psychopath, I started visiting on Tuesdays and Thursdays, when Jacob was in preschool. I played piano for them. I brought in nail polish to paint the old women's nails crazy colors, and soon even the men were asking me to paint their nails. There was a one-legged ninety-eight-year-old woman who was sharp as a tack. She invited me to her room and showed me photos of her family.

"They only visit twice a year," she said.

"Is there anything I can do for you?" I asked.

She said, "I'm dreaming of a doughnut."

I loved this. "What kind?"

"One from Dunkin Donuts, with the jelly inside."

"Why can't you have one?" I inquired. I couldn't imagine why they wouldn't give this ninety-eight-year-old a doughnut.

She said, "I'm diabetic. That's why I don't have a leg."

Okay, so she was diabetic. But she was ninety-eight years old! On my next visit, I brought her five doughnuts. She said, "I'm going to eat them after lights-out," and hid them under her pillow.

Once the residents learned that I would take any request, I was regularly sneaking in doughnuts and other forbidden treats. I had something in common with them: I knew how it felt to wait to die. A couple of ladies took me to their rooms and told me about their families and their lives. It seemed to me that the greatest loneliness of aging was feeling like you didn't have a voice. These women had stories to tell, and I listened. I didn't talk about myself; they weren't interested in me. They wanted to be heard.

Now that both kids were in school, I also had some time to think about myself. For the first time I had a social life—my friends who lived nearby would come over to watch *Mad Men* or *Nurse Jackie* after they put their kids to bed. Sometimes I'd meet up with my friend Kate, the wife of our former pediatrician from Charlotte. Coincidentally, they had moved to West Hartford right before we did, so I had a built-in friend. Kate was smart and sarcastic, the kind of irreverent mom who didn't make a big deal out of giving her kids a coffee or a Coke if they asked. "You want to try it? Have it," she'd say.

We saw other mothers giving her dirty looks, but Kate didn't care. Once, when she had a bad day, she showed up at our house in the middle of the day with a bottle of wine and announced, "I can't take it anymore. This is for us bitches."

When I was sick, I'd lost seventy pounds, most of which needed to go, but I had no muscle, just lots of extra, sagging skin. Besides walking everywhere in my hometown in Poland, I had never exercised in my life. I wasn't allowed to. After playing piano through high school, I entered the music conservatory, where I practiced eight to ten hours a day. The teachers at the school were responsible for producing musicians who could compete at the highest level, so they made sure I didn't play sports and risk injuring my fingers.

Now Kate dragged me to the gym at the local JCC. The first time I went to an exercise class, I was very self-conscious. Everyone around me was in shape and knew exactly what they were doing. But I started with the smallest weights and dutifully went three times a week. A couple months later I noticed muscles I'd never seen before and gained some confidence. In the gym's mirrors, I saw that the other women looked like a million bucks in their matching workout clothes while I wore Russel's old, stretched-out T-shirts. I'd started gaining muscle and looked healthy, and I wanted to show it, to feel good about myself when I left the house. I hadn't thought about such things for what felt like a lifetime. It was, in fact, Nathaniel's lifetime.

I went to the same class three times a week at the JCC, religiously. It was called Group Power. The instructor was on stage with a microphone. She looked so strong. I had mental strength, and now I wanted physical strength to match it. The stronger I got, the better I felt.

I became addicted to my workout, and when I get excited about something, I like to set a high, almost impossible goal. Two years after my very first class, I decided I wanted to teach the Group Power class. It was a specific program run by a company called Mossa. I flew to their headquarters in Atlanta for a weekend and went through the instructor training. After submitting videos of myself leading the class, I passed the assessment. This was a huge milestone in my life. I had been sick and weak, and now I was healthy and strong—I felt like I could move a mountain, and I'd found a new way of making myself feel better. To pass the assessment, I'd also had to prove I could memorize the hour-long routine and speak clear enough English that the class could follow my direction. I was proud of myself.

I wasn't the only one who was rebounding from those hard years. Russel remembers seeing a photo of himself from right after we moved to Connecticut. He was sitting on the couch with a slice of pizza in his hand and a beer resting on his big belly. He tells me that when I saw that picture, I said, "You're disgusting."

A few nights later a set of mail-order DVDs arrived at the house. Russel had seen a commercial for an exercise regime called P90X. It promised him that he could be buff if he just followed the program. He quit smoking and drinking, built a little gym in our basement, and went for it. Six days a week, an hour and a half a day. In forty-five days he lost twenty-something pounds, and he kept going, continuing to work out and changing the way he ate. When he traveled for work, he brought exercise bands and went to the hotel gym. Now Russel goes through phases of getting into great shape then taking a break and complaining about his health, but when we both got in shape in Connecticut, it was a milestone. It felt good to both of us to be so fit and healthy after my life had been on the line.

Russel's office was only a few miles from our house. Every morning before school, I'd put Jacob in the stroller and Nathaniel would grab his scooter to walk Russel to the bus. Then, at the end of the day, he'd call and say "I'm leaving the office now. I'm on the 5:48 bus. I'll be at Farmington Avenue at 6:02."

As his bus pulled up, I'd see Russel looking out the window, eager to see us. When friends asked him to play golf or go out after work, he mostly turned them down. He was just loving being a father and being with his family. He told me he felt like he was becoming more of the man he had always wanted to be, a better version of himself.

At home, in the evenings, I was back to reading novels like I had my entire life except for the previous six years. Sometimes, after the kids were asleep, I would leave Russel with them while I wandered around Marshalls, for the first time in a long time having the leisure to shop for shoes. (In Poland, when I was little, we only ever had one pair of shoes at a time, and we wore them until they had holes in the soles. Here, there are so many shoes to choose from. I still can't get over it.) Being away from my kids every now and then helped me be a better mom, and I was finally clear-headed enough to seek out what I needed: exercise, friends, the chance to give back, and a little retail therapy.

All the not-normal of our lives was starting to look pretty normal. A kid with physical challenges, different on the outside but in school, learning to read, and playing with the neighborhood kids. A mother with cancer, in remission, finding new interests.

In certain ways we'd been dealt a bad hand, but it didn't break us. It didn't break my faith in God. It made us stronger. Nathaniel fought to breathe, to eat, to see, and to hear, though he might never be able to smell. I found new appreciation for how remarkable these bodily functions are, and how effortlessly most of us live.

Nathaniel experienced his senses differently: He never had the experience of losing functionality. He didn't go from breathing easily to needing a trach; he didn't lose his hearing. Instead, he was on a path from restriction to freedom, in many ways the same as growing up is for most kids. A baby goes from milk to baby food to solids. Nathaniel went from being fed by tube to eating real food. Every child has to learn to watch out for hot stovetops, stay out of the street, and hold their breath under water. Nathaniel had a few more items on that checklist, but the process, the growing cognizance and self-care, was a familiar trajectory. That's how I saw it and how I presented it to him. Nathaniel wasn't a victim; none of us were. That wasn't part of his or our family's identity.

## 17. shallow water

I could have stayed in that life indefinitely, but after three years in Connecticut Russel took another job back in North Carolina. It was a move that made sense; the position was a step up the corporate ladder. Jacob was now six—he'd started kindergarten—and Nathaniel was eight. The schools in Charlotte were good, Russel's parents were still there, and it was more affordable.

On Nathaniel's last day of school in Connecticut, his classmates, teachers, and nurses presented him with a memory album filled with notes and pictures. His nurse, Lisa, and Dr. DePalma all had tears in their eyes.

We moved back to the same cookie-cutter neighborhood we'd lived in before, but a different section. We bought a house that was a similar model to the one we'd sold, but this one cost less because the real estate market had gone down. Most of our medical bills were paid off for the time being, and Russel was making more money, so our finances were no longer an everyday worry.

Summers in Charlotte were steamy, and families gravitated to the community pool. It was the kind of place a kid could happily spend all day every day: There was an Olympic-sized pool, a kiddie pool for toddlers with mushroom-like water features, and a huge waterslide surrounded by a lazy river. On Fridays the pool was open until 10:30 at night, and families would order pizza and eat poolside.

Most of the kids around Nathaniel's age were good enough swimmers to play in the main pool, and they'd go down the waterslide over and over again. Nathaniel was dying to go down the waterslide like the others, but it wasn't safe for him. If water got into his trach, it would go straight to his lungs, and he could end up with pneumonia, which happened all the time during cold and flu season. The first weekend the pool was open for the summer, Russel stood at the bottom of the slide, catching him before he went underwater. But then Russel went back to work and that Monday, I tried to take over. I waited at the end of the slide, with water up to my chest, for my fifty-five-pound son to barrel into me. He came down with a crash—I had caught him!—and when I stood up the top of my bikini was completely off and slowly sinking. Holding him above the water by his armpits, I somehow maneuvered and managed to rescue my top. Then, using Nathaniel as a cover-up, I carried him to the side of the pool and quickly put my top back on.

When I looked back up, I noticed the teenage lifeguard looking at me. "I'm sorry there's not much to see," I said.

He blushed.

That was the first and last time I did the waterslide with

Nathaniel. After observing my exchange with the lifeguard, Nathaniel said, "I'll never ask you to catch me again. If Daddy's not around, I'm not doing it."

He was mostly a trouper about the stuff he couldn't do. He'd just say, "I don't want to go to the pool," but we knew it bothered him. How could it not?

For Jacob's sixth birthday, he really, really wanted to rent a bouncy house with a waterslide. Maybe he wanted it because he loved waterslides, or maybe a tiny part of him suspected his big brother wouldn't be able to participate and the attention could finally be on him. We were acutely aware of how Nathaniel's needs affected Jacob's childhood on a daily basis. If ever a sibling could say that his childhood was "unfair," it was Jacob. His whole schedule revolved around Nathaniel's medical needs. Back when Nathaniel still had a g-tube and we'd be stuck in the house feeding him, my mother-in-law gave Jacob little pots and pans, measuring cups, and other brightly colored cooking tools. He had a special drawer labeled "Jacob's cooking drawer." He was enthusiastic about this activity, but it wasn't necessarily his first choice. Thankfully, whether by good fortune or in reaction to his situation, he was a people pleaser.

For this birthday party, we decided we wouldn't deprive Jacob of a waterslide if it was what he really wanted, so we rented an inflatable one for the front yard. It hooked up to a garden hose at the top, and water flowed continuously down the side.

Just before all the kids were supposed to arrive, Nathaniel begged to take a turn on the slide. The pool at the bottom was very shallow so he wouldn't even need someone to catch him. He tightened the cap on his trach and had a go. But the minute he plunged to the bottom, his trach filled with water and Russel had to suction him. The cap was attached by a Velcro tie and it just wasn't a perfect seal. We told him that it was too dangerous and, unfortunately, he couldn't go down the waterslide again.

This time Nathaniel got upset. He'd been anticipating the fun of the slide, and we'd all thought he'd probably be able to do it. After all, it was smaller than the slide at the pool—just an inflatable toy—and he'd always had inflatables for his birthday. We didn't realize that this one would be so different. Now Jacob was having a fun party and he wouldn't get to be part of it.

Nathaniel screamed, "It's not fair; take that slide back! I don't want it in my yard!"

Then Jacob got upset. Because his birthday was in the middle of the summer and that was when we scheduled Nathaniel's surgeries, Jacob rarely got to have a real party. It was supposed to be Jacob's day.

Russel turned to me and said, "Get Nathaniel out of here. Whatever it takes. Let his brother enjoy himself."

I took Nathaniel to a go-cart track for the rest of the party, promising him and Jacob that we'd come back in time for the cake. When Nathaniel and I left, Russel went inside the house to hide that he was crying because he hated the fact that we couldn't enjoy birthdays together like a "normal" family.

While Nathaniel accepted his limitations most of the time, there were other occasions, like the waterslide, when he wasn't happy that other kids could do things he couldn't. We managed those on a case-by-case basis, deciding when we felt he should suck it up and accept it and when we felt he deserved our sympathy.

For example, when all the other neighborhood kids started riding bikes, I pushed him to join them. Every kid should know how to ride and I didn't want him to miss out. We lived on a long, safe street, and that's what the kids did all summer. But Nathaniel wasn't enthusiastic and part of his resistance had to do with the helmet. It didn't fit over his hearing aid, and yet it wasn't safe (or fun) for him to ride without being able to hear. Russel tried to cut a piece out of the helmet, but the trach was right in the spot where the strap fastened. Then I bought a small helmet that didn't interfere with the hearing aid, but because of his small chin, the strap kept slipping forward.

As far as Nathaniel was concerned, the solution was easy: He could ride without a helmet. But I wasn't about to let him do that. His next proposal was to return to his recumbent three-wheeled bike that that was so low to the ground it could be ridden without a helmet, but I wanted him to ride a two-wheeler, which I felt was an important part of growing up. So I made him wear the annoying tiny helmet that looked like a yarmulke. Since it was unlikely to do any good, I ran alongside him as he biked, ready to catch him at any moment. Needless to say, wearing a yarmulke-looking helmet while your mother runs alongside your bike was not exactly a thrilling scenario for a young boy who just wanted to play with his friends. He'd complain, cry, and call me unfair, but I insisted.

Sometimes he wanted to use his difference as an out, like when it came to tying his shoes. He was lazy and refused to do it. Jacob, who was seven, was able to tie his shoes, as were their friends, so I insisted that Nathaniel learn. I didn't want him to be an adult, out with friends, having to ask someone to tie his sneakers so he could play tennis. I couldn't see him wearing Crocs and only Crocs to college.

# 18. good christian neighbors

This time around, Charlotte was hard for me. Maybe because the school principal there was younger and less experienced, when we suggested writing a letter to the parents of Nathaniel's classmates, she said, "Okay, sounds good." That was it, meeting over. She duly forwarded the note we'd written, but we'd been spoiled by Dr. De-Palma. Nathaniel's new principal didn't take interest in his well-being (it was unclear if she even recognized me when she saw me at school), but the other parents were warm and welcoming.

Because I'd lived there before, I thought that I knew what to expect from our neighbors, but one woman ruined it for me.

Our house was in a gated community with 600 houses, each with a similar layout but painted different colors. There were lots of kids who all played together. Directly across the street from our house lived a boy named Luke who was Nathaniel's age. When the neighborhood kids played in a group, Nathaniel and this kid got along just fine, but it soon became clear that his mother, Liz, had problems with my son.

They had a trampoline in their backyard, which we could see from the upstairs balcony of our house. One day Nathaniel spotted a bunch of neighborhood kids playing there. He went over and rang the doorbell.

Liz came to the door and said, "We didn't make plans for a playdate today, Nathaniel." I could hear her from our doorway. She used a friendly, authoritative mom voice. "We'll make plans another day." Then she sent him away as if this were how the world worked and he just didn't know it yet.

Nathaniel came home crying. There were no other kids left for Nathaniel to play with. They were all gathered at that one house.

At school the next day, Luke told Nathaniel that he wanted to be friends but his mother wouldn't let him. Nathaniel was a sweet kid—not violent, rude, or destructive—so it was clear that the only reason she had shunned him was that she was uncomfortable with the way he looked. I had infinite understanding for any child having this reaction—a young person might need some time and guidance to get used to Nathaniel. But in this case, the boy wasn't the issue. His mother was the one who couldn't handle it. As an adult, that was her burden to bear, but she placed that burden on my child. It was incomprehensible.

When it was Luke's birthday, Liz went so far as to arrange two parties. One was at her house and included Nathaniel. Another took place outside the house—maybe they went bowling or to a play space, I didn't know. What I did know was that Nathaniel wasn't invited to the second party, even though every other kid in the neighborhood was. This absolutely mystified us.

Russel, who is the opposite of shy, asked her directly. "Why did you invite my kid to one party and not the other?"

She said, "It's my son's special day. If Nathaniel were there it would take attention away from him."

When I heard that, I was speechless.

Russel and I had the conversations you'd expect: Maybe we're imagining this. Maybe Luke wasn't available when Nathaniel rang the doorbell, but his schedule changed. Maybe there was only room for a limited number of guests at the second party. Then Nathaniel befriended another neighborhood kid, Jake. Jake had Duchenne muscular dystrophy, a difficult, progressive disease. Russel found out from Jake's father that Liz treated Jake exactly the same way. It was an oddly validating moment, to have another parent of a disabled child say, "You're kidding me. You too?" This woman was truly shielding her kid from Nathaniel and Jake because they were different.

We tried to address it in a civilized fashion. There was a conversation in their home. Liz said, "Being friends with Nathaniel is just too intense for Luke. I don't want him to have to deal with that." She tried to justify limiting their time together, to us and, I think, to herself.

The tipping point came when Russel arrived home one day to find Nathaniel and me both upset over another exclusion. He went upstairs to the balcony and watched for Liz's husband to show up. When he did, Russel went over to their house, got up in his face, and yelled, "You'd better talk to your wife! My son is hysterically crying because of her and the way she treats him. He doesn't have enough to deal with? Now I have to worry about this?"

The whole neighborhood could hear what was going on — I could see them peeking out of doorways and around hedges.

Russel went on, "She claims she's a good Christian. You married an evil bitch. I'm not going to touch her, but I'm going to beat the shit out of you if she doesn't stop treating my son like dirt."

I was embarrassed. "Please stop," I told Russel and dragged him back to our house.

As we passed their next-door neighbor, he said, "Good for you, Russel, I hate that woman."

Liz was the only person who ever made Nathaniel cry. She was deeply religious and went to church every Sunday, and yet, outside church, she lived by a logic that would never make sense to me. If Nathaniel had a surgery, she'd tell me that she'd prayed for me, as if being a good Christian made the rest of her behavior toward him unassailable. But I've met a lot of amazing Christian people. Karen, a friend from our first stint in Charlotte, had true Christian values. She checked on me every day, offered to help with the kids, and truly cared about me. When I was declared cancer-free, she showed up with her family and brought a cake. My next-door neighbor Diane was always kind to me. She was into being healthy and knew I was too, so she brought over smoothies that she made in her Vitamix and invited me to jog with her. But Liz's treatment of Nathaniel made me want to sell our house and move away.

I ended up going over and apologizing to Liz and her husband for Russel's behavior. But knowing that any day she might do something to hurt Nathaniel shaped my days.

One of my neighbors often asked me to join her in an afternoon glass of wine before the kids came home from school. This always sounded like a perfect way to take my focus off Liz. One glass turned into two, sometimes more. Life was better when I had a bottle of wine, but it was an artificial solution. When the children arrived, I was already a little tipsy, which made me too self-absorbed to care about the details of their days. I lived on the surface, where nothing hurt.

Eventually, I asked God for the strength to stop drinking. The period of my children being little and dependent on me would be so short and I didn't want to miss it. We didn't need exotic vacations, horseback riding lessons, or French classes; all I wanted was to have a real connection, where we could talk and know each other. So we did: We went online together to research what makes people successful. We talked about drug and alcohol abuse. I pampered them by giving them baths, one at a time, while I sat on the edge of the tub and heard about their days. We didn't need more than that.

We persevered. We got a dog. I taught exercise classes. There were plenty of distractions, and I tried my best to face us in a different direction and to empower Nathaniel. I worked hard to give him a normal social life, hosting make-your-own-pizza parties and cooking dinner for all the neighborhood kids. And I have to admit I bought him the most coveted toys to give him a leg up on making friends.

In the afternoon, Nathaniel would ride his miniature jeep in a loop around the neighborhood. Every kid wanted a ride on that jeep. One day a kid crashed it into a wall, and after that Nathaniel wouldn't let anyone else drive, but he was happy to chauffeur them around. I couldn't control my neighbor, but I could put my son in the driver's seat.

## 19. a marathon, not a sprint

Dr. Bernstein, Nathaniel's ENT at NYU, was a true gentleman. He dressed immaculately. He had a calm, assuring voice. And he had very soft hands. Whenever I shook hands with him, my hands felt like sandpaper compared to his. Jenna and I joked that we'd have a crush on him if we weren't all married. Our last visit to Dr. Bernstein had been while we were still living in Connecticut. He had already tried more than five or six times to open up Nathaniel's airway, without success. During that last appointment, a month before we moved back to North Carolina, we sat in his office to discuss what next steps we might take to try again, but before we got very far, he stopped.

He said, "Russel, Magda, when I became a doctor, I took the

Hippocratic oath: First, do no harm. But I have fallen in love with your son. I'm too close to him, and because of that I can no longer give you an unbiased medical opinion as to his treatment. I find myself discarding options because they're too risky, but another doctor might see the risks more objectively. Nathaniel's case is complex; maybe there is someone better for him out there."

Dr. Bernstein sent us to Dr. Robin Cotton at Cincinnati Children's Hospital, who he said was "the" guy in the world of ear, nose, and throat doctors. Working with him was a doctor named Kaalan Johnson who was completing a fellowship in pediatric otolaryngology. Our ultimate goal was still to achieve the breakthrough that the doctor in Charlotte was attempting when he accidentally poked a hole in Nathaniel's brain. (I swear I won't mention that again.)

Drs. Cotton and Johnson and their team carefully mapped out the bone structure of Nathaniel's face to make sure no such thing happened again. They spent over a year gathering data, taking CT scans, tracking Nathaniel's growth, and planning for the surgery. *Surgeries.* They told us he would have one big surgery, to open his airway. It was the most complex procedure he'd had up to that point. Then there would be eight to ten smaller follow-up surgeries to repeatedly clear away the scar tissue and new bone that would immediately threaten to fill the hole that the doctors created. If you looked at it from the outside, it seemed so simple: All they wanted to do was to open a bone blockage in his nose. But the structures in his face were so close and out of whack compared to a normal person's that there was a significant risk of damaging his vision or brain.

We couldn't afford to fly from Charlotte to Cincinnati for all those appointments, so we made the ten-hour drive many times over the course of a year. Sometimes Jacob and our cockapoo, Smokey, stayed at my in-laws' while Russel and I did the long drive with Nathaniel, but usually I stayed home while Russel took him.

When my kids were little I told them to open their imaginations to the hidden worlds that were all around us, and on those car trips I saw that pay off. To pass the time, Nathaniel invented a warrior combat team. All the kids in the neighborhood had specific roles and powers, and their shared goal was to defend Cincinnati from evil forces. His imagination was his refuge when he was bored, a decent substitute for playing with his friends. Then, when we got home from seeing the doctors, he'd fill the kids in on the status of their battle, and they would all disappear for hours to continue their story.

Growing up in Poland, we had a TV, but there wasn't any children's programming so I turned to books for entertainment. I consumed all forty-seven of a Scandinavian fantasy series called *The Legend of the Ice People*. Tellingly, in their witchy culture, every time a child was born, the mother would die. (It was only when I had my own children that I recognized that as a metaphor.) There was a good prince in those books, a hero with superpowers, whom I fell in love with. His name was Nathaniel, and that's where I got the idea that one day I would have a son and name him Nathaniel.

Now that real boy, the namesake of the boy in the books that had inspired me, was writing his own legends. I'll never forget the day I drove us to Cincinnati in crazy pouring rain. It was so torrential that I wondered if I was putting us in danger by making the trip. But the appointment was already scheduled and Russel had taken time off work to be with Jacob, so rescheduling seemed more difficult than powering through.

Nathaniel spent the entire ten-plus hours regaling me with the story of one single, epic battle. It was raining so hard that I could barely see the road, and I wanted to focus on my driving instead of Nathaniel's story. Silently, I prayed for a pause, perhaps a nap, maybe a quiet musical interlude. But no, only as we finally reached our destination was Cincinnati saved!

Of course, I knew these games were a vital escape from boredom and distraction from the medical world. That's why I wasn't exactly surprised that when the doctor asked Nathaniel if he had any questions about the surgery, Nathaniel politely asked if they could give him Spider-Man fingers at the same time as they worked on his nose.

The day of the big surgery finally arrived. It was during Nathaniel's winter break from third grade. We drove up from Charlotte and checked in to the same Embassy Suites we'd stayed at during the preparations. It was in Covington, Kentucky, right near a bridge that crossed the Ohio River into Cincinnati. In the middle of the hotel lobby was a large cage hosting Emmy, the resident male (yes, male) parrot, with whom Nathaniel always loved to have (rather limited) conversations.

We were all very experienced OR visitors by this point; we had it down to a science. As we headed through a pediatric hospital to the pre-op room, we would pass other rooms in which parents were waiting with their children. You could see panic on their faces, even for a tonsillectomy. In contrast, our pre-op room was always a lively show. Whenever Nathaniel was going under general anesthesia, we'd take advantage of it by squeezing in multiple procedures, so within the hour before surgery it was like Grand Central Station in there. We might have a gastroenterologist, an anesthesiologist, a craniofacial surgeon, a general surgeon, an ENT, a plastic surgeon, and a dental specialist all rotating through to check on Nathaniel.

Sitting on my lap, Nathaniel would politely acknowledge them then go back to playing on his Nintendo DS. The hospital had plenty of video games for kids to play, but Nathaniel always returned to Mario on his DS. Russel would be in surgical garb, ready to escort him to the OR. He'd talk to everyone, somehow reaffirming details of the procedures and asking questions about their spouses and kids at the same time.

When Nathaniel began getting nervous, he'd start some superhero narrative. Meanwhile, I'd try not to be distracted by the image of his little body in that big room surrounded by all those strangers, and the fear of everything that could go wrong. I'd nod my head and ask about the superheroes, "And what was that one's power?"

"Mom, I *just* told you."

*Nathaniel: Once when I was little, I had a surgery scheduled for 11:00 a.m. You can't eat for eight hours (or drink clear fluids like water or apple juice for five hours) before general anesthesia, so the last meal I'd had was dinner the night before. The surgery was delayed . . . and delayed and delayed. We were waiting in a boring pre-op room and I couldn't eat the whole time. Finally, they told us the surgery had been rescheduled for 4:00 p.m. So not only did we have several more hours to wait in the boring room, but I still wasn't allowed to eat. Dad was really mad. I could see that he was about to give the nurses a piece of his mind. I was hungry, and for some reason I was craving Indian food. But I figured if there was a delay there was probably a good reason. I was pretty sure the doctor wasn't sitting in an ice cream parlor, having trouble deciding which flavor he wanted to order.*

*I said, "Dad, if the doctors are late there is probably a little boy in the operating room who needs them more than me. I'm fine, Daddy, we can wait."*

Remembering Nathaniel's patience in that moment always makes Russel cry. When he cried, as he often did, or got angry, I rolled my eyes, feeling a little embarrassed. I usually don't show emotions; I'm only cuddly with my children and dogs. That's how I was raised. My parents are the same way.

Americans tend to judge intelligence by how educated people are. And, to generalize even further, globally thinkers often congregate in big cities to collaborate and promote their ideas. But in the part of Poland where I grew up, close to the Ukraine border, for a long time there was no chance of higher education. For generations, my family has been farmers. The Communist government was strict about what was taught in school. We didn't even learn the full scope of history in grade school—we just learned pro-Communism history.

But what we lacked in education, we made up for in street smarts. Or, more accurately, it fell on the women in particular to be the intellectual pillars of the family. Mothers used the dinner table as a place to instruct their sons on how to behave and what to do. Women were wise and strong leaders of the household, but the way they led was through their sons. They were the brains behind the men's hands. My grandmother was functionally illiterate, but she guided our family. Everything my family has—the land, the house, the drive to be educated—we have because of her.

She raised seven kids in the middle of nowhere, and every one of them went to university.

I saw emotions as weakness, and it was important to me to be strong for my son. I didn't want Nathaniel to see me cry before surgery, and I wanted to appear tough to the doctors and nurses, so I put up a shield. It took me a while to get there—I cried a lot during the first year or so of Nathaniel's life—but after that I told myself it was time to step up. I had no more tears left to cry.

I had no excuse to pity myself—I wasn't the one going through surgery—and I wasn't going to pity him because I didn't want him to feel sorry for himself. Maybe it's those Polish farmer genes, but Nathaniel turned out like me. He doesn't get emotional. He doesn't cry. He is tough, like a rock. I tell him it's okay to show emotions, but that's the way he is. He tells himself, *This is how it's going to happen, and I'll get through it.*

Russel's emotions come from going down the path of "what if." *What if Nathaniel had been born without differences? What if something goes wrong in surgery today?* I am more pragmatic; I don't do "what if." But the upside to Russel's intensity is that he is always connected. The cliché is that a father who has to earn enough money to support the huge medical costs of a family like ours would check out, making the office his domain and leaving not just the household work, but also the household *feelings* to his partner. Russel was *in it* as much as I was. Furthermore, he counterbalanced my tough shell by making friends left and right, wherever we went. Then, in emergencies, when I couldn't keep it together, we switched roles entirely: I fell apart, and he was the rock.

From the time Nathaniel was a baby, whenever he's had surgery, Russel gets into a gown and carries him from the pre-op room into the OR.

By now, the doctors and nurses at the hospital knew all our rituals. There was one woman with pink hair who sat at the front desk who knew how much I liked warm blankets and always brought them to me. She didn't have to do that, but she did. She also knew I slept through every surgery. When Russel took Nathaniel into the OR, she pointed to a corner and said, "That's the quietest area. Go to your spot and take a break!"

The hospital might have fourteen operating rooms, and Nathaniel is inevitably in the one at the end of a long hallway. Russel swears that as he carries Nathaniel, the hallway gets longer, and, skinny as Nathaniel is, the stress makes Russel break a sweat. In his father's arms, Nathaniel goofs around, which is his way of taking himself to some other place, but he never ever resists or makes a fuss.

*Nathaniel: For some reason, on the way to the hospital room my legs feel like toothpicks and I can't stand on them, so my dad carries me. It's always the same. The OR is a big room, all cold metal and machines. There's a viewing balcony and giant flat-screen TVs with images of my skeleton. There are huge lights, and white sheets draped over the trays of knives and scissors. I guess they don't want me to see the tools they'll be using to destroy — I mean improve — me. There might be six to ten medical professionals in scrubs, playing with knobs on various machines. Once we're in the operating room, Dad sits on the table with me on his lap, ready to attach the gas to my trach. The gas is what puts me to sleep for the surgery, and I'm always nervous to take it. It doesn't hurt, but knowing I'm being put under makes me feel kind of sick, so that's when I bring out my best delay tactics. I ask every doctor in the room about their roles, what all the machines are, why there are pink beads in the anesthesia machine, etc. I'm at my most inquisitive when I'm stalling. Dad lets me hold things up for a bit, but eventually I take a deep breath and tell him I'm ready. He sits with me on his lap while they hook the gas up to my trach.*

The doctors are taught to watch for physical phases as the anesthetic knocks the patient out. I'm never in the OR, but Russel tells me that the anesthesiologists always get a kick out of Nathaniel's narration of his own condition. He walks them through every stage that marks his progress: "My voice is starting to change. My muscles are starting to feel stiff."

The anesthesiologist turns to Russel and says, "He's giving me the play by play!"

*Nathaniel: When the IV first goes in, I feel fine, and then it kicks in all at once. I know in five seconds it will ram me.*

*Sounds start morphing from echo-y to robotic.*

*It's almost like I'm watching a video of me talking—I know what I'm saying but can't quite control it.*

*Then Dad's hands feel clammy.*

*Then I start feeling like it's not happening.*

*Then I get really dizzy and start to slur my words.*

*Then I fall asleep.*

Just before Nathaniel goes out, his body fights it for a split second. Part of the reason I'm never in the OR is that Russel doesn't want me to see this part. It's hard to watch your son's body be taken over by drugs. Every surgery is risky, and it's always scary.

Once Nathaniel is under, Russel lays him down, takes off his hearing aid, walks out of the OR, and collapses. But I only know this because Russel has told me. By the time he gets back to the family waiting room, I am already completely out. It doesn't matter how small or uncomfortable the chair is, I fall dead asleep the minute Russel carries Nathaniel away. Sleeping is how I deal with stress, and for the most part it's a good coping strategy: It's hard to show weakness when you're asleep! I don't get up to eat. I don't need to go to the bathroom. No matter how long the surgery lasts, there I am, covered in blankets, sleeping through the entire thing until Russel shakes me to tell me the doctor is on his way to tell us how it went.

> *Nathaniel: I always wake up from surgery angry. It must be a side effect of the anesthesia. Of course, I can't hear because they've taken out my hearing aid, and I've never liked that. But instead of politely asking for it back, I'm full of rage. Once I punched a nurse who tried to hold my hand. I've been known to try to rip out an IV. Even though I always have to stay in the hospital to recover, and I know this, I still wake up saying, "I just want to go home. I don't want to be here anymore." Five minutes later I've calmed down and am ready to move from the recovery room to a patient room, usually on a different floor.*

Dr. Cotton supervised, and Dr. Johnson performed most of the surgery. They went very slowly, a millimeter at a time, watching everything they were doing on a screen. We thought it would take six hours, but it ended up taking eighteen. The stamina of the doctors was incredible.

We had hope that finally getting his nose open would mean we could take the trach out, but we knew it wasn't likely. His breathing did improve but his airway wasn't large enough to let in enough air. Even so, there was now a light at the end of the tunnel. Dr. Johnson promised us it was the first step of a long journey, still cause for celebration.

We now had to be vigilant about preserving the hole the doctor had made. As was the plan, Nathaniel needed a number of smaller follow-up surgeries to repeatedly clear away the scar tissue, so we returned to Cincinnati every four weeks at first, then at longer intervals. It was a family priority.

At our final appointment in Cincinnati, Dr. Johnson told us he had some news to share. He had been new to the hospital when we'd first met him and had helped Nathaniel throughout this latest medical adventure. He announced, "I'm moving to Seattle Children's hospital." We thought that meant that when Nathaniel had his next surgery, Dr. Johnson wouldn't be part of it. Little did we know that three years later this doctor would become a huge part of our lives.

*part three*

## wonder

## 20. a "real-life" auggie

In February of 2012, when Nathaniel was eight, the book *Wonder* by R.J. Palacio was published. *Wonder* is a novel about a ten-year-old boy named Auggie Pullman who has craniofacial issues very similar to Nathaniel's. The book begins when, after having been homeschooled through many surgeries, Auggie goes to his neighborhood school for the first time in fifth grade. Told from Auggie's perspective and that of the people around him, the book is funny and moving and real. It has, at its core, a message of acceptance and kindness that does the miraculous: It really stays with kids.

Russel read *Wonder* in one day and found the similarities to our lives uncanny. The parallels were not just familiar—it felt like the author knew our lives. He immediately called our friend Nurse Pat to tell her about this amazing book.

Pat said, "Are you kidding me? The author is sitting across the room from me right this minute." Apparently, when R.J. was researching the book, she had visited the medical center to meet with experts on Treacher Collins. The first thing she saw when she walked through the door was a huge picture of Nathaniel hanging on the wall, so she'd known about Nathaniel for a long time. Right after that phone call, Pat put R.J. and Russel in touch.

I knew, vaguely, that Russel was emailing with R.J., but before I could give it much thought, I had an unpleasant surprise.

I had gotten certified to teach the Mossa fitness program at the studio in Connecticut, but we moved back to North Carolina before I had the chance to put my training to work. Luckily, Mossa is used in health clubs around the world, including in Charlotte, so I finally started working as an instructor. I led a Group Power workout. The instructors wore shirts that said "Power," which spoke to me.

For the first time in a long time, I was the center of attention. In a faraway lifetime, I had been a performer. As a pianist, I had been accustomed to having people watch and listen to me, and I liked it. Attention in the form of the stares Nathaniel drew was unpleasant, but to my surprise, I discovered that I had missed being center stage. I quickly became one of the more popular instructors, with a devoted group of followers. In class, between exercises, there was very little time to talk personally, but I tried to squeeze in bits of inspiration: "You guys, if you can believe it, I was in a wheelchair three years ago. I had a fractured spine. I found fitness, and I feel better mentally and physically. I'm stronger than I've ever been." My students saw me as proof that anyone could get into shape. Over time, they emerged from corners of the room to share their own stories.

Mossa creates a program of specific routines that instructors follow internationally, and they send out the new routines via video. The way I've always motivated myself is by setting high, if not impossible goals. My long-term goal for Nathaniel was to get rid of his trach. The ambitious goal I set for myself was to become one of the video instructors. When there was a call for applicants, I submitted a video of myself teaching class. I was really excited when I was named a finalist in their search. This was exactly what I needed now that the boys were in school and stable—a part of my life that was just for me.

I was filming another video of myself teaching class for the next round of the competition when something went wrong. I started to squat and my body locked; I couldn't go lower. I said, "You know what guys? Something is wrong. I think I pulled a muscle. I can't squat, but you should go all the way down."

It was the strangest thing, and it had come on suddenly, like a snap of the fingers. At the end of the class I limped out, bewildered.

My doctor's office happened to be around the corner from the gym so I went straight there. He took an X ray, then showed me that where the ball of my hip was supposed to be, there was only a shadow.

"How are you walking around?" he asked.

"How am I missing a hip?" I answered.

It turned out that the cancer tumors had caused nerve damage, which was why I wasn't feeling any pain, and I had avascular necrosis—there wasn't enough blood flow to my hips so the bone tissue in one of them had died. They told me it was a somewhat rare side effect of the steroids in the chemo cocktail I'd had six years earlier. Lucky me!

I needed a total hip replacement immediately. Like, yesterday. The doctor said that if I happened to fall, I would end up in a wheelchair for the rest of my life. I went from teaching a workout and lifting weights one day to bedrest the next—no walking allowed.

I was angry. I was only thirty-four. I'd just beaten cancer and found the joy of fitness. So much for my dream of becoming a video instructor.

"You're not going to have a hip replacement done by someone mediocre," Russel said. "You need to go to the best doctor." We'd had such a bad experience with Nathaniel's surgery in North Carolina that we were irrationally gun-shy about all the local doctors, many of whom were surely top-notch. We decided I would have the surgery in New York, where if the doctors were counting on Jesus to guide their hands, they knew better than to say so.

We found a surgeon recommended by our now numerous medical connections. The operation would cost $20,000 in cash that we didn't have, a huge financial burden. We didn't indulge in luxuries (except for Nathaniel's toy jeep), and Russel worked hard at his job. But for all this working and saving, we were broke. People who suffer physically get the special bonus gift of financial suffering.

We made plans to meet R.J., the author of *Wonder*, when we were in New York to see the hip surgeon for the first time. Of course, Russel had cried the whole way through the book, but I hadn't read it yet. Before we left home, I'd tried to start it, but the truth is that I picked it up, read a few pages, and knew I wasn't ready. Dealing with Nathaniel's Treacher Collins was a daily struggle. I was still so deep in it that I wasn't ready to reflect on it. The book was too close to home.

The New York doctor affirmed the no-longer-shocking news that my hip was shot. We scheduled the surgery. Like the first doctor, he didn't want me walking around at all.

So, when I crutched myself into the cute West Village restaurant to meet R.J., my mind wasn't on *Wonder*. I was mentally preparing for my own big surgery, scared and full of self-pity. But R.J.'s warmth and kindness was captivating. She told us what inspired her to write the book. She and her kids had gone into an ice cream shop in Brooklyn and had seen a child with Treacher Collins. Her younger child had a bad reaction. Unsure how to handle the situation, she hurried them away from the store.

I figured out right away that the child they'd seen was Emily. "I know that family," I said. "I know Emily and her mother, Jenna. Jenna helped me cope when I was first digesting Nathaniel's situation. She's the most amazing person I've ever met."

I told R.J. that her child's reaction was understandable and that it had even been hard for me to meet Emily. She said, "I'm still not okay with my reaction. It wasn't my child's fault. I was the one who pulled him away."

I thought, *This woman is brave.* Talking to me, the mother of a son with the same condition, R.J. didn't make excuses. She took responsibility for her actions.

"I couldn't let go of what I'd done," she told me. "I felt like I owed this mother and this girl an apology, so I wrote it in the form of the book."

Sure, her hurried flight from the ice cream store hadn't been ideal, but it wasn't anything new to me. I saw it all the time: the shocked faces of people, their unfiltered reactions. Finally, one of them had done something about it! R.J. was humble, honest, and pure. She wanted to change, and by writing *Wonder* she did something to help millions of people change. It was beautiful.

At that time *Wonder* was newly published, and R.J. told us that so far it had sold 1,600 copies, not an enormous number. She was giving presentations at schools and libraries, trying to spread her message through story. In her meetings with students, they were very curious about what Auggie looked like. R.J. told us that Nathaniel was in her head when she created Auggie, remembering the photo she'd seen of him when she first walked into the hospital. But she didn't know anything else about him, so she was struck when we told her how many details of our lives she'd captured in her book. Later, when Nathaniel started joining her for appearances at schools and other places, she would say, "Nathaniel Newman is Auggie Pullman come to life."

It was easy to connect with R.J.—she never felt like a stranger —but at that first meeting we had no idea how important the book would be to us, to the craniofacial community, and to a whole generation of kids.

Forty-eight hours after hip replacement surgery they throw you out of the hospital. To our relief, myFace, the organization that helps kids with craniofacial differences, stepped in. They own an apartment in New York City where kids visiting doctors can stay free of charge. It happened to be empty, so they let me recover there for three extra days.

There's a risk of blood clots if you fly too soon after surgery, so we drove back to North Carolina. I was nowhere near ready for the trip, but I was antsy to get home. We had left the kids with my sister Agnieszka, a physical therapist, and Russel's mother was also there to help out. But we'd already been gone for five days, which was four days longer than we'd ever both left the children at the same time. I had only been apart from Nathaniel a handful of times in his eight years of life, and even then I had the comfort of knowing Russel was home with Nathaniel.

I couldn't sit up in a chair yet, much less in the passenger seat of a car for a nine-hour drive, so Russel folded down the rear seats of our SUV and created a hospital bed for me using an air mattress, a sleeping bag, and some pillows. After several hours of driving, we were both very hungry and in need of a bathroom break. Russel pulled into a strip mall with a Starbucks to buy sandwiches, backing the truck into a space right in front of the outdoor cafe. When he opened the hatch to hand me a sandwich, all the people drinking their coffees turned as one to stare at us. There I was, woozy and pale, propped up in our makeshift mini-ambulette. Who knows what stories they made up in their heads to explain why a man was feeding a clearly drugged-up woman who was lying, incapacitated, in the trunk of his car.

Eight weeks later I was back on stage, teaching aerobics. My glute muscle was entirely gone—it looked like I had only one butt cheek—but I was a stronger instructor for the experience. I taught a class for all fitness levels, and again I told them what I'd been through, the list now a tiny bit longer: "I wasn't allowed to exercise growing up because I was a piano player and the teachers didn't want me to injure my fingers. Nowadays I love to feel strong, but my body's broken. My spine was cracked. My hip bone disintegrated. For a while I had a tough time doing cardio because I had cancer tumors pressing against my heart. My body isn't perfect and strong, but it has carried me through hell."

I wanted my students to think, *If she can do it, I can too.*


## 21. the boy from the *wonder* book

Nathaniel had become a spokesperson for myFace, and Russel was on the board, so we frequently ran into R.J. at craniofacial events. Though fictional Auggie and real-life Nathaniel had a lot in common, there was one way in which they were very different: Auggie wanted to hide his face. He often wore a space helmet, and Halloween was his favorite holiday because in his mask he was just like everyone else. So far—and he's fifteen, so things are looking pretty good—Nathaniel has never wanted to hide his face. He's always known he is different, and people have always stared or done a double take when they first see him. Nonetheless, he is proud of who he is, and he wouldn't want Treacher Collins taken away from him. It's part, but not all, of who he is.

One year, close to Halloween, Russel took the boys to get frozen yogurt in Charlotte. Nathaniel was about eight. They were sitting outside, eating the yogurt, when a man—a fully grown adult man—came up to Nathaniel and said, "Wow, where did you get such a cool mask? I wish I had a mask like that for Halloween." His tone was mocking and he looked proud, as if he'd just made the funniest joke in the world.

Russel saw red. As he started to erupt, Nathaniel looked that man in the eyes, smiled, and said, "It's not a mask. It's my face!" Then he turned back to his frozen treat and devoured it with passion. A few nights later, he trick-or-treated with more energy and enthusiasm than any ten kids could've summoned.

I take some credit for this attitude. When I was growing up, I read a book about the Polish piano prodigy Frederic Chopin. When he first performed publicly, at age eight, the audience that witnessed his genius went wild. His mother, seeing that he was overwhelmed by the adulation, didn't want him to think of himself as such a standout. She told him, "You are wearing a beautiful suit. They can't get over how handsome you are in this suit."

I remembered that, and whenever Nathaniel asked, "Why are they staring at me?" I wouldn't say, "Because your face is unusual." I'd say, "You're handsome. People are fascinated by your face. Everybody else looks like each other, but your eyes are different, you don't have cheekbones, and you have almost no ears. They're curious, and they wonder, 'Where did this special boy come from?'"

At night, when we were brushing teeth, I'd stand in front of the mirror with him. "Look at you, what do you think about your face?"

"Nothing."

I said, "Touch your eyes, they're beautiful and big. Look at your hair, it's lovely."

I'm sure some people would expect me to say to him, "Let's talk about what happened today. How did that make you feel?" when there was an unpleasant incident. But most of the time I didn't mention it. Instead of assuming he was upset and helping him talk about his thoughts and feelings, I chose to model that it was no big deal. I didn't expect him to be injured by other people's bad behavior and ignorance, and I didn't want him to dwell on it.

The only person who hurt him tremendously was Liz, the neighbor who had told her son not to play with Nathaniel. Then, the only time I saw my son crying because of someone else's cruelty, we talked about it.

"I know it hurts. You can't change that woman, and we can't either. We tried talking to her, but she didn't listen, and I think she's making a big mistake. But you have other friends, and other people don't decide who you are as a person. Make sure you're a good person in your heart, and, if you can, forgive her. She's insecure, and you shouldn't take it out on yourself." It didn't seem to help Nathaniel much in that moment. He couldn't even catch his breath — he never cried like that.

It's hard for me to remember how I used to talk to people with visible disabilities before Nathaniel, but now I am completely open and maybe even too friendly because of the connection I feel with them. Once at Lululemon, I met a temporary employee, a young guy with a huge scar across his face. I said, "I know we just met, but do you mind explaining what happened to you?"

He smiled immediately and said, "Oh my gosh, you are the first person who has actually asked. There's a story behind this scar, but if nobody asks, I never get a chance to tell it. I was in a terrible car accident. I'm happy to be alive, and my scar is a reminder of how lucky I am."

Of course, not everyone is always in the mood to talk, and it's not their responsibility to answer my questions. But having Nathaniel taught me that one thing is certain: It's better to ask than to stare or be rude.

*Nathaniel: Around kindergarten or first grade I saw the movie* Shrek *for the first time. I was already obsessed with superheroes, and Shrek rose above them all. It's been pointed out to me that Shrek, who is fat and green and dirty, is still portrayed as a hero. He likes the way he looks, and only when the standard beautiful princess is transformed into her true ogre self does he love her. It's been suggested to me that, as a little kid, identifying with Shrek was the easiest way for me to embrace the idea that I didn't have to be perfect on the outside to be a good guy. It's a clever idea. It makes sense. I get it. Shrek equals me. But people around me want everything to be about my differences. Can't I just love a great movie?* Shrek *has an 88 percent approval rating on Rotten Tomatoes; maybe I'm just part of that 88 percent. People look to Treacher Collins as the characteristic that defines me, but I don't see everything through that lens. I don't even wear glasses.*

Not long after we met R.J. Palacio, Russel took a new job in New York, and we had to move again. We left North Carolina for New Jersey when Jacob was almost seven and Nathaniel was nine. Leaving our Charlotte neighborhood—especially Liz—gave me a new burst of energy.

Russel quickly found a pretty house in Maplewood, New Jersey. Coming from our cookie-cutter neighborhood to a town where everything was old and overpriced wasn't going to be an easy transition, but this house was perfect! We put an offer in on it, but it failed the inspection. Turned out it was infested with black mold. When that deal fell through, we decided to rent. Russel was commuting to work, and one day he called and said, "Guess what! I found a rental. It's a cute little house, and the boys can walk to school."

Russel is the consummate salesman. The house he described ended up being three houses off a busy highway. It looked out on the garbage area of a supermarket, and across the street was a shopping center. The location was noisy and unpleasant, but he was right: The boys could walk to school.

That Christmas in New Jersey I started working part time at Lululemon during the holiday rush. I chose Lululemon because when I was about to have my hip replacement, Russel had gone to the one in Charlotte to treat me to a high-end workout outfit. Their philosophy is to create real relationships with people who walk into the store, and Russel told the friendly salesperson about me, and that I was about to have surgery. The store took interest in my plight, and right before my operation, they took photos with me to promote a new line of clothing. Then, when I was still in the hospital recovering, they sent me a video they'd made about how inspirational I was. It made me feel special, and I resolved to work there one day.

Working at Lululemon allowed me to try different gyms—they pay for their employees to do so—and connect with the community. I brought home a little extra money, half of which we used to pay bills, and the rest of which went into savings accounts that I opened for the boys.

Our cockapoo, Smokey, had never been alone for long stretches of time. Now when I left for work, I'd see him sitting in the bay window at the front of the house, waiting for our return with a mournful look in his eyes. When we arrived home, he would be in the exact same place, still waiting. We decided that Smokey deserved a companion.

We needed a hypoallergenic dog—fur and trachs don't mix —and I found a website for a place in Pennsylvania Amish country where they had cockapoo puppies. At the time, I was ignorant about puppy mills (breeding operations where all they care about is making money and the puppies are treated inhumanely).

Russel, the boys, and I drove three hours to the address I'd been given and came to an oddly empty house. It was clear that nobody lived there. Then an Amish man in his thirties appeared. Acting as if this was his home, he mentioned his wife and children and said that everyone was working. Something was off. Only later would I realize that he'd probably had us meet him there instead of at a huge, filthy warehouse stuffed with hundreds of dogs.

Nonetheless, he went inside and returned with two cute puppies, releasing them to tumble and jump on the grass. He picked one up. "This is yours."

This was definitely not the dog I'd seen in the picture online, a cockapoo named Monica. This was a mixed breed dog. A shedding dog. Possibly a golden retriever/Chihuahua mix.

Russel said, "That's not a cockapoo."

The guy said, "You don't want it, leave."

But it was too late. The boys were already fawning over the dog.

Coco was sweet and good, and Smokey loved her. She was the first female dog we'd had, and the boys treated her like their baby, dressing her in pink tutus and choosing pink plushies for her at the pet store. She even had a pink bed. We'd never had pink around the house. Now we had a spoiled baby girl.

Every day we walked to school with the two dogs. The boys' classmates would pet Coco and say, "She's so cute! What kind of dog is she?" We told them she was an Amish cockapoo.

Smokey still sat at the bay window waiting for us to come home, but now Coco was right there next to him, and the mournful look was gone from his eyes.

In New Jersey, we were just a twenty-minute train ride from Manhattan, and we played tourists. We went to see *Spider-Man* on Broadway. We visited the Statue of Liberty. When Nathaniel was younger, he had loved to scramble on the rocks in Central Park. Now he could do so without hurrying back to NYU for a doctor's appointment.

I had walked past the Empire State Building innumerable times when Nathaniel was a baby and we were living in Hoboken. It was on my route from the subway to the hospital, the route that had been such a struggle with a stroller in winter. I'd never had the time and leisure to go up to the observation deck on the 102nd floor, but now I took the boys. It was the first time they'd been anywhere so high, and they were quiet as they took in the whole city from above: how big everything was, how the water surrounding it showed that it really was an island.

As for me, looking down, I saw the tiny, blurred heads of passersby and I remembered when I was one of those specks on that same street, eight years earlier. How much fear and pain had been invisibly knotted in my small form, twisting through my cells, rotting into cancer. Each person who happened to be on the street as I gazed down on them was a question mark, an unknown story of struggle and hope. There was no telling if, how, or when one of their stories might intersect mine.

Not long after we moved to New Jersey, I was stopped at a red light in the middle of town when someone rear-ended us.

Nathaniel screamed, "What was that?"

I flew out of the car, furious. "What's wrong with you? How can you drive like that? I have children in the car! Why weren't you paying attention?"

A young woman stepped slowly from her car. She was probably in her early twenties, and very thin. She didn't look healthy. I immediately knew there was something going on; I recognized her from a world that I knew. My anger dissolved.

She said, "I'm so sorry. I'm on my way to the doctor. I reached down to get my papers."

I said, "No, it's okay. We're all okay. The car doesn't matter."

She told me that she had colon cancer, and as she spoke I saw that she had a chemo port in her chest. "I just got married, but I'm not going to survive this."

Life, death, all around us. I had survived, and Nathaniel was thriving. I was grateful to God. I silently renewed my resolution to be mindful of every interaction, to remember what was important, and to do my part to make the world a gentler place.

*Nathaniel: When we moved to New Jersey, R.J. contacted us and said, "I'm going to talk at a private school on the Upper West Side. Do you think you could join me?"*

*It may sound strange, but reading* Wonder *was not a monumental occasion for me. (Confession: No book is really a mon-*

*umental occasion for me.) In fact, Jacob had a bigger reaction than I did. He was in second grade when he read* Wonder *for the first time, and, like Dad, he read it all in one sitting. Jacob was excited by the similarities between me and Auggie: How Auggie, like me, had one true friend instead of lots of friends. And how we both loved Star Wars. And our dogs. How Auggie struggled with everyday things: eating, making friends, being in dusty situations, not being able to swim.*

*Where Jacob saw the similarities, I tended to see the differences. People expect me to identify with Auggie, and get all emotional and cry like my dad. But to me, though Auggie has medical issues that are similar to mine, he has a completely different personality.*

*But then, when I started to see what people were getting from the book, and how it was actually changing their behavior toward me, that's when I understood how powerful the book is. That was monumental.*

*When I did that first school visit with R.J., I sat at the front of the stage with my mom, Jacob, and R.J., and her husband was in the audience. The fourth-grade class gathered in front of us — they had already read the book and were there to meet a "real-life Auggie." I didn't know what questions to expect, but a lot of kids asked, "Does it hurt? Were you in a fire? What happened to you?" One kid asked, "Are you in a special class for special kids?"*

*I don't mind when people ask how I acquired these facial features, although ideally they could put the question aside and just get to know me. What I really don't like is when the questions jump to assumptions. Being asked if I was in a fire, or if I'm in a special class rubs me wrong. It's like saying, "Hi, nice to meet you. Have you ever fallen down a hole?" Or "Why is your hair brown?" I don't spend time wondering, much less asking, why someone looks a particular way. There's an answer, but does it need to be known? It doesn't matter and it's not my business.*

*I visited schools to support R.J. and the book, and because it was kind of fun, but in my day-to-day life I don't want to be seen as Auggie Pullman, or "the real Wonder boy." First of all, I'm not the only kid with Treacher Collins, and secondly, I just want to be seen as Nathaniel Newman. I want to be seen as a normal kid who happens to look different.*

## 22. reno

We had only been in New Jersey for a year when the CFO at Russel's company got caught cooking the books and the company went bankrupt. Russel lost his job. He quickly found another . . . but it was in Reno, Nevada. I couldn't believe we had just uprooted our family, only to have to move again. We flew to Reno to consider the opportunity, and his new boss took us to dinner in a casino restaurant.

"You'll be happy here," he told me. "There's a small-town vibe."

After a dinner of hearing from the boss and his wife how great our new life would be, I was sold. The offer was very alluring. We could pay off all our debts and finally relax a little. Russel promised that we could build my dream house. I liked the sound of that.

We bought a lot facing the mountains and rented an apartment to stay in while the house was being built. I started leading workouts again, this time for a New Zealand–based company called

Les Mills, and I continued working at Lululemon (thank God for chain businesses!). On weekends we explored as a family, driving to San Francisco or Lake Tahoe, or taking Smokey and Coco on hikes. Life was good.

Nathaniel was unfazed by the move, just as he'd been with the others. He's a laid-back kid, and wherever we went he always found one good friend, usually an outsider like him, and that was all he needed. Oddly, because of his special needs, there was a certain consistency to his life. We always introduced him to his new class with a letter, as we'd done when he started kindergarten. He always had a nurse accompanying him to school. He always had doctors' appointments, pleasant or not, which gave structure to his time. Moreover, because of his medical needs, there was a certain amount of attention he still required from me and Russel.

Jacob's salvation was sports, and he found his best friends on the teams he joined in every new city. It was hard for Jacob to leave Charlotte, where he had three very close friends, but coincidentally they were all moving away too, so it would have been just as bad for him to be left behind. During our year in New Jersey, the greatest thing that happened for Jacob was that he discovered and fell in love with lacrosse. In Reno we signed Jacob up for lacrosse right away. When I think back on our time there, one of my best memories is the spectacular fields where Jacob played. In New Jersey, North Carolina, and Connecticut, all of the East Coast parks I had seen were surrounded by houses and streets, trees and forests. You couldn't see much beyond the field itself. But in Reno, you could see miles and miles of desert in every direction from any field. When Jacob practiced, usually at an elementary school, Nathaniel would climb and make friends at the playground, and I would perch on a bench with a view of both boys. The open fields that stretched into the beyond captured my imagination. It was the most geographically enchanting place I've ever lived.

Driving in Reno you also see endless desert stretching before you. The mountains in Poland were very different. My town, which was built on top of a hill, surrounded a castle the likes of which Reno has never seen, though there is no shortage of McMansions. A river ran along the foot of that hill, and my family lived on the far side of the river. You could see a tall mountain range in the near distance, but mostly the area was hilly and lush, and changed color with the seasons. The houses in town were tiny, each with a neat fence in front, a well-tended garden, and hand-painted flowers on the doors. It was folksy and charming, with enchanted forests full of nooks and crannies where mythical creatures might be hiding.

In the desert of Reno, the open spaces felt completely different. The space was expansive; you could travel in any direction. The remote horizon was never-ending and seemed to say you can go anywhere, you can be anything, the possibilities are endless.

I had just finished a yoga class when the phone call came. Russel told me awful news. Coco had been hit by a car and had died. I burst into tears. (I'm pretty good at repressing my emotions, but we all have our limits.) Somehow I made it home, where Smokey was licking Coco, trying to wake her up. I was crazed with grief. In my mind there was only one thing to do: find another dog exactly like Coco and bring her back to our apartment.

Nathaniel: Mom came home and took me to an animal shelter to try to find a replacement for Coco. The same day she died! Mom wasn't really thinking straight. She started looking for another dog that looked exactly like Coco, but it was really like she was hoping to find Coco herself. Like I said, Mom was kind of hysterical. I watched her cry and thought, I have to make sure she doesn't get a dog today.

I tried to comfort her, saying, "Coco's in heaven now, let's just go home."

Meanwhile, she was looking at all the dogs, saying, "This dog shakes his tail just like Coco . . . the eyes look like Coco . . . the coloring . . ." We spent about two hours there, searching hopelessly.

Then my mom went to the front desk and said, "Are there more dogs? I'm looking for my dog." She described Coco, and the rescue workers clearly thought she was actually looking for a lost dog, because they took us from the adoption side of the shelter to the other side, where they had dogs who had been found on the street and weren't yet up for adoption. My mom fell in love with a pair of Brittany spaniels who looked a lot like Coco.

Finally I said, "Please, let's go home," and dragged her out of there.

The house felt empty and quiet without Coco. Smokey wouldn't eat. I couldn't bear seeing him alone. Three days later, after I had semi-recovered my senses, I brought Smokey with me to a pet store. I told the guy my story, and that I was looking for another cockapoo.

"We only have one cockapoo, and she's kind of sick."

He showed me a puppy in a cage. She was the only dog who wasn't eagerly leaping toward me, wagging her tail and hoping I would take her home. She was just lying there in her own filth. Her eyes were gooey. I wanted her.

"How much is she?" I asked.

The guy told me her price. It was very high, especially for this poor, sick dog.

"I'll give you half," I countered.

He replied, "I'll give you that price if you have lunch with me."

I was shocked. "I'm married and I've been crying for three days and you're hitting on me? What kind of person are you?"

By the time I was done scolding him, I had my dog at my price. No lunch date. When I brought the puppy home, I told the boys to think of it as though Coco's sacrifice brought us Snowball.

The boys had never experienced death before, and they had different reactions to the loss of Coco. Jacob talked about her often, and when Russel took them to a children's museum, Jacob brought home a blue pillow with buttons on it and "Coco" written on it with a Sharpie. He slept with that pillow every night. Once, when the other dogs (soon to join the family) got ahold of the Coco pillow and tore a hole in it, Jacob carried on like someone had died. I found a sewing kit and fixed it, and from then on Jacob kept it hidden under the pillow on his bed.

Unlike his brother, Nathaniel didn't talk about Coco much, but he would look at pictures of her and feel sad. Coco was in our hearts, but we had to focus on the living. Together, we read a poem about a pet crossing a rainbow bridge into a beautiful meadow where he would frolic until his owner joined him. Nathaniel seemed to take that image to heart. In his mind, Coco was up in heaven, waiting for him.

Snowball seemed to know best how to help Nathaniel heal. Every night, when he went to bed, Snowball got under the covers with him and waited until he fell asleep. Then she came to let me know that her work there was done, and she was ready to do the same for me.

## 23. hollywood

At first we didn't take much notice of the change *Wonder* was precipitating in the world. I was preoccupied with my own life: Recovering from surgery. Moving to New Jersey. Moving to Reno. Raising the kids. We knew it as a story, we adored R.J., and we liked helping to spread the word.

Then something changed. A tipping point. R.J.'s book had become a bestseller. Strangers on the street started saying to Nathaniel, "Oh, have you read *Wonder*? You look like the boy from that book."

Nathaniel or I would answer, "We did read the book, and we know the author." These seemingly trivial exchanges marked something truly miraculous. Part of why seeing Nathaniel for the first time made people uncomfortable was that they didn't know what to make of him. What was going on with this kid? Was he okay? What should they think of him? How should they react? They didn't know what questions to ask to help them understand him. Maybe things changed because they now had a picture of Auggie in their heads, or maybe just seeing a boy whose face was different sparked the connection. Either way, it was to *Wonder*'s credit.

Practically overnight, the book gave what seemed like an entire generation of kids a way to process Nathaniel's face and the idea that there was a real, likeable person behind it. Obviously, this wasn't just about Nathaniel. It applied to other kids with Treacher Collins, and anybody with a craniofacial condition. It turned out that brilliant blue-jacketed book and its message was all those kids ever needed to understand my son. Nathaniel still got stared at, but not as often as when he was little, and these stares were different. Kids were curious, but they didn't react fearfully and run away. Parents were now more willing to come up and ask me questions.

In Reno, when Russel and Nathaniel wrote the letter introducing Nathaniel to his classmates, it said, "You've probably read the book *Wonder*. That book is about a boy who is just like me."

*Wonder* didn't change us, but it dramatically changed how other people approached us, and in that way, it changed our lives. *Wonder* made the world feel like a friendlier place.

Around Thanksgiving of 2014, just before we left New Jersey for Reno, Russel and R.J. talked. She mentioned that there was going to be a movie of *Wonder*. They already had a director and a screenwriter, and she had proposed that Nathaniel play the main character. "He's my real-life Auggie," she said. "That's how I picture him." The producers flew Nathaniel from Reno to LA and gave him a script with a couple of scenes to practice.

*Nathaniel: The audition was kind of like taking a test. I memorized my lines. I tried to put feeling into it without overacting or underacting. But there's also improvisation; it's not the same as just taking someone else's words and character and making them come to life. At one point I got confused. We were doing a scene where Auggie gets kicked out of the library. (I don't think the scene ended up in the movie.) The woman playing the librarian told me to leave. I wasn't prepared for that—I didn't know if she was saying her line, or if she really wanted me to get off the stage. I figured they didn't actually want me to leave, so at first I just stood there. She told me to leave again, this time more harshly, so I walked out of the room. Then she asked, "Where are you going?" Yeah, I wasn't a pro. After it was over, everyone told me I'd done a fine job—they all knew I wasn't coming in as a professional—and they told us they were a long way away from making final decisions about casting.*

*Wonder* was now being taught in schools nationwide. At his new school in Reno, Nathaniel's teacher told someone in her book group that she had "a *Wonder* kid" in her class. Word spread from there to Elizabeth Vargas, a host on the ABC news show 20/20. Elizabeth was interested in doing a segment with our family about Nathaniel and wanted to meet us.

The next time Russel went to New York on a business trip, he had lunch with the 20/20 producers and Elizabeth. They went to a fancy Midtown restaurant that was the unofficial ABC cafeteria. (The movie and 20/20 both fell somewhere under the Disney umbrella.) As they ate lunch, various onscreen personalities came over to greet Elizabeth.

Elizabeth wanted to explore a part of our story that wasn't central to *Wonder*: the challenge of giving a kid with severe differences the opportunity to have a normal life. Russel was sold, and we agreed to do some preliminary interviews with the producers so they could get a sense of us as a family. We'd done something like this before: a short documentary for the National Geographic show *Taboo*. All of us assumed that 20/20 would do something similar, a short "slice of life" profile. Which is what they would have done . . . if our lives had gone on as they were.

*part four*

# the big one

## 24. a unique form of torture

God works in mysterious ways. In 2015, not long after we moved to Reno, we decided that the best medical team for Nathaniel was conveniently located in Seattle. Some of our New York team was retiring, and they told us that Dr. Richard Hopper at Seattle Children's was the best in the world. Most compelling was that Dr. Hopper was pioneering a new surgery that might allow Nathaniel to get rid of the trach. For good.

In a stroke of good fortune, Dr. Hopper was working with Dr. Johnson, who already knew Nathaniel from Cincinnati. When Dr. Johnson told us he was moving to Seattle, we'd thought we'd never see him again. We'd had no idea he'd end up working with Dr. Hopper to develop a new surgical approach to help people like Nathaniel breathe normally.

I had been so anxious about moving to Reno, so far from NYU and the doctors who had shepherded Nathaniel his whole life. But God brought us to the West Coast, and that was exactly where we needed to be: an hour-and-a-half direct flight from Seattle Children's hospital.

•  •  •

The doctors in Cincinnati had opened Nathaniel's nasal passage, but he still couldn't take in enough air without the trach. If this new procedure was successful, Nathaniel would finally be able to breathe like everyone else. myFace did the math for us. He was eleven years old, and he had already had fifty-five surgeries totaling $1.7 million. Removing the trach was something we'd been striving toward his whole life. To be able to go to school without a nurse. To be able to take a bus. To play without fear of dislodging it. To shower by himself instead of being bathed by me. To swim with the other kids. It was the biggest step toward normal we could imagine for him (and, frankly, for us).

Dr. Hopper said, "You'll hate what I'm going to tell you; it's draconian." He and his team planned to address not just Nathaniel's jaw—which we had already expanded through five distractions over the years—but the structure of his entire face. It would take several preparatory surgeries, and then the biggest one was a whopper, not just because of the eleven-hour surgery itself, but because of what came after.

The follow-up treatment, which would expand his face, was not very different from what you would invent to torture your worst enemy. (Sure, when you torture your worst enemy, the goal usually isn't to improve his breathing, but otherwise this was exactly the same.) After the surgery, Nathaniel would have a heavy framework (we called it the "halo" or the "cage") around his head with sixteen screws that were mounted to his face in various places. Five of those screws needed to be turned one or two millimeters every day. He would wake up from surgery with his eyes sewn shut, his jaws wired closed, a g-tube in his stomach, and the halo on his head, and he would face months of being mostly confined to bed. In the beginning he wouldn't be able to eat, see, or talk, which pretty much eliminated almost every way a bedridden person might keep himself sane during the long weeks of recovery.

In the end, if the surgery was successful, Nathaniel's face would be shaped differently. He would still look like himself, Dr. Hopper promised us, but there would be room for him to breathe. He explained, "The entire process, including six surgeries, will take a year to a year and a half, but we might be able to get the trach out." Nathaniel would be only the third child to ever have this procedure. It was as if the doctors, among themselves, had said, "If we can fix Nathaniel Newman, we can fix anyone."

The description of the treatment was not a pleasant thing for a parent to hear. I wondered how it was sounding to the eleven-year-old would-be patient. This wasn't something we could inflict on our son against his will. It was barbaric. That was why we'd brought Nathaniel with us to Dr. Hopper's office to hear everything he had to say. "You're doing this because we said so" wouldn't fly. He couldn't wake up surprised to find his head in a vice. He had to know what he was getting himself into, and he had to be on board.

When the doctor finished describing this terrible but potentially miraculous plan, Russel and I looked at our son to see his reaction. Nathaniel was in the corner of the room, with a sheet of paper taped to his chest. He'd colored the paper red, and there were big holes stabbed through it, as if he'd been riddled with bullets.

"What are you doing?" we asked him. I think we both expected him to say, "This is what you want to do to me. You're going to destroy me."

Instead, he said cheerfully, "You're not going to believe it. We've been overrun by monkeys, and they all have muskets."

Nathaniel had always found his way through the pain and suffering, and this was exactly how he did it. Monkeys and muskets one day, a superhero or two another, these characters made mayhem in his head, their comic book battles distracting him from bad news, boredom, and pain.

Russel pressed him. "Nathaniel, this is serious. It's going to suck. Did you hear the details? Do you have any questions? What do you think?"

He said, "Do I get to miss school?"

Russel said, "Yes, you'll miss three months."

He gave me a double thumbs-up. "Awesome. Let's do it."

*Nathaniel: I was bored. To be honest, I'm always bored when doctors are talking, but my parents make me turn off my iPad when there's "stuff I need to hear." So I had asked a nurse for a marker. The one she gave me happened to be red. While I "listened," I drew a bullet hole on a piece of paper and taped it to myself. Did it mean I had a death wish? No! Occasionally I draw laser beams going through people. This doesn't mean I'm violent or insane. It just means I like the way I draw laser beams.*

*For my whole life I'd known my trach was a danger to my health and a huge inconvenience. But it was also all I'd ever known. It felt normal to me. Imagine if someone came up to you and said, "Wow, you have to go to the bathroom several times a day? Your body doesn't just take care of that on its own? I feel sorry for you; that must be gross and annoying." And when you looked around, you saw that nobody else had to interrupt what they were doing to take a bathroom break. You* were the only one. Nobody else even had bathrooms in their houses, so you had to carry around special equipment to handle your unusual needs.

Then you might say, "Okay, I get it. Their bodies work better than mine." You would understand that idea, but it would still be hard to actually know what it felt like for your body to work just like theirs, what it felt like to be "normal."

Every superhero has a weakness. Mine was my trach, and one of the worst things about it was that I couldn't swim. Or the doctors told me I couldn't swim. In Reno, at the neighborhood pool, I decided I would find a way to go underwater. I pushed the trach back and tightened the cap as tight as I could. I'm gonna try this, I thought.

"Dad," I said, "I'm going under water."

Dad said, "You gotta risk it to get a biscuit."

My mom isn't quite as open to breaking the rules. She'll say, "You shouldn't do that," and then she'll watch, worried, ready to jump in and save me, but she doesn't go so far as to make me stop.

So I ducked my head under. It was only for a second, but when I came up, I was like, Yeah, I did it! Whoa! I felt happy and proud. I was being brave. I didn't care what the doctor would say . . . as long as he didn't know.

I said, "Dad, I went under water and I was fine."

"You did?" he said. Then I showed him.

Even though I could only do it for a second, I liked being underwater better than being above it. I ducked beneath the surface over and over again. The only downside of this version of swimming was that . . . it didn't really work. I couldn't stay under more than a second, and water got into my trach once or twice when the band didn't stay as tight as it needed *to be. Also, this act of bravery guaranteed that I would need to change my trach tie because it got soggy. So, yeah, the reality was that I still couldn't go under water. But at least I knew I had tried and gone as far as I possibly could.*

*When I said, "Awesome! Let's do it!" I was acting like the surgery was no big deal, but I really did like the possibility of being able to swim farther, deeper, for longer, without an adult hovering nearby. And though it was hard to imagine, I knew that if I didn't have a trach, so many of the medical issues I dealt with every day would just . . . disappear. I wouldn't get infections. I wouldn't worry about someone bumping into the trach. My parents wouldn't have to change the tie that held it in place. I wouldn't have to get a new trach every two weeks. The trach cap wouldn't pop out and fly down the school hallway when I sneezed, like it once had done in front of my whole class. I liked what the surgery promised, and I wanted to have it and for it to be successful, but I didn't want to get my hopes up.*

The two children Dr. Hopper had performed the surgery on were a baby and an eleven-year-old girl named Izzy. At one of those first meetings with the team in Seattle, Dr. Hopper told us that Izzy and her family were in the hospital for an appointment that day. He said, "Let me ask them if they're willing to talk to you guys. When you go to lunch, I'll text you." But as we were leaving his office, we ran into them in the waiting room. Izzy had the cage on her head. It looked very dramatic, but she was smiling.

Russel said, "Hey, this is Nathaniel, he's going to have the same surgery that you had."

They were gentle, kind, and warm. Izzy couldn't talk with the cage on, but she was clearly in good spirits. Her mother confided to me, "This is the hardest thing we've ever done, but I think it's going to work." Izzy's breathing had improved. Not long after that, she would successfully have her trach removed and be able to eat for the first time in her life without using a g-tube. This was the best news we could imagine.

Plans for Nathaniel's surgery were solidifying, and the movie people still hadn't told me if they wanted Nathaniel to play Auggie. Getting the role was a long shot, but I felt I had to let them know our schedule just in case. Walking the dogs one day, I picked up the phone and called Todd Lieberman, the producer we knew best.

"I realize that you're putting a lot of money into this movie and your schedule doesn't revolve around one boy," I said, "but I don't live in your world. I'm just a mom, and I wanted to let you know that we're scheduling a surgery that will change Nathaniel's life. It'd be amazing if Nathaniel or another kid with Treacher Collins could play Auggie. It would be authentic, and it would bring great exposure to the craniofacial community. We're here to help if there's anything we can do, but this surgery is our priority."

Todd thanked me and told me the movie was already moving ahead. He then said they had someone in mind for the role.

A couple days later Todd called Russel. He said, "We got the kid from *Room* to play the role. Jacob Tremblay. He's a great actor." We hadn't seen *Room*, but Russel and I watched it that weekend. During the movie we kept looking at each other and saying, "Wow, this kid is amazing. He'll be so awesome playing Auggie." We were blown away.

The next time I talked to Todd I told him he'd made a wise decision. Sure, it would have been great to give the part to someone with a craniofacial condition instead of a "normal" person wearing a prosthetic and makeup. But their goal was to make an amazing movie, and the more successful they were, the bigger a spotlight would shine not just on the craniofacial community, but on R.J.'s universal message of accepting difference and choosing kindness.

In preparation for the big surgery, we flew up to Seattle every two to three months for testing and procedures. We scheduled it for March of 2015, expecting the worst part to be the first three months at least, during which Nathaniel would be wearing that heavy halo.

One day about four months before, right around Thanksgiving, I was feeling anxious about the surgery. I shut down when I get anxious, so since the kids were at school, I was lying in bed with the dogs, reading a book. At 11:15 I heard the front door open. The dogs jumped off the bed, excited, as Russel walked in, a weird sarcastic smile on his face.

"What are you doing home?" I asked.

He said, "I just got fired."

I figured he was joking. "You're not feeling well?"

"No," he said, "No, this asshole fired me. He called me in and said, 'It's been great having you. The board has decided to go in another direction. We're letting you go.'"

We had only been in Reno for one year. Russel had never been fired—he'd never even gotten a negative review. In fact, he'd just been given a raise. He reminded his boss what was going on with Nathaniel. How could they fire him thirty days before Christmas, and four months before his son went through the biggest surgery any kid could have?

The COO of his company said, "Yeah, I know it's hard. But

we're giving you six months' severance and a year of health insurance."

Now, being a salesman, Russel had a pitch ready for me. "God smiled on us," he told me. "I'm getting paid for six months, and I can focus on Nathaniel full time."

I felt a line of electricity radiate from the top of my head, down through my face, to my throat, and all the way to my stomach, shocking me inch by inch. I started hyperventilating; I was having a panic attack. "What are we going to do now? I can't believe this. What kind of luck is this? We lost Coco. We built a house. We have a mortgage. Nathaniel's having surgery. We can't live without health insurance!"

What really got me was that I hadn't wanted to move to Reno in the first place. At the restaurant Russel's boss took us to when he was wooing him, he told me, "I had the same cancer as you." He'd had lymphoma. He and his wife talked about how Jesus had carried him through cancer.

After that, when I talked to my mother about the move, she had said, "Yes, you should go. They are Catholic, they have good hearts."

I had trusted these people. They let us down so badly.

Christmas and Hanukkah came and went. The surgery was two months away. Russel was home every day, lifting weights and looking for a job. Then he got a phone call from Brian Griffith, one of his closest friends from the job he'd had in West Hartford.

Brian said, "I heard you're out of work. How come you didn't call me? Come work for me; I'll create a position for you." They wanted Russel to start right away, but they were very accommodating and agreed he could start on May 15, after Nathaniel had been recovering for a month. The only caveat was that we would eventually have to move back to Connecticut, but that was a while away.

All was good. Russel was still getting paid by his old job; he could stay home and help Nathaniel through surgery; and his new job would be ready and waiting as soon as we knew Nathaniel was stable. Brian was an angel among us.

We had agreed to let 20/20 do a profile of our family to coincide with the release of the *Wonder* movie. We felt honored to represent the community. The film crew wasn't intrusive—in the beginning they did more following than interviewing. They went with Nathaniel to the playground. They came hiking with us and the dogs. And they spent time at our house, watching our daily routine.

When we first started talking with them a year and a half earlier, we were just beginning to explore the possibility of having the halo surgery. The only plan at that point was to talk about the movie release and show a kid who had a similar life. But now it morphed into *Wow, this major surgery is insane!* Instead of finishing our interviews before the procedure, 20/20 decided to make it a more in-depth story, following our family for a couple of *years*, leading up to and including Nathaniel's major surgery.

For the first nine months or so, we worked with a team of producers who were getting to know us and shooting B-roll—extra footage of us going about our lives to complement the interviews. Then Elizabeth Vargas came to Reno. She didn't just sit down and ask us questions. She accompanied Nathaniel to a trampoline park and went ziplining with him in Lake Tahoe. She came to my Body Pump class. She put her whole heart in the project. We were both mothers of two sons and fitness lovers, and I felt a real connection with her.

## 25. a dog angel

*Nathaniel: In Seattle, the night before the big surgery, I was allowed to eat whatever I wanted. It would be the last meal I tasted for four months. Four months! We went to an Italian restaurant and I ordered a big plate of fettucine Alfredo and a huge piece of cheesecake. Our appointment at the hospital was at six o'clock the next morning.*

It was March 22, 2016. The surgery started at 8:00 a.m. and lasted more than eleven hours. Dr. Johnson came out of the OR first. He told us that Nathaniel had come through, and that he was pleased with the results. Dr. Hopper was finishing up. 20/20 wanted to film us when we first saw him, but Russel and I said we preferred to be alone.

Nathaniel was still asleep when we went into the recovery room. He wasn't super swollen yet—that would come later. He had a cage mounted onto his face and skull, just like the one we'd seen on Izzy. It was difficult to look at, but his face was still that of our beautiful Nathaniel. I hadn't expected him to look so peaceful.

We left his room and told the 20/20 cameras what we'd seen and how we felt. Then we said goodbye to the crew and were still right outside the door to the PICU when Dr. Hopper and Dr. Johnson emerged. It had been four hours since they finished the surgery. Nathaniel was still asleep, and they'd just checked on him for the last time before going home to get some much-needed rest.

They told us, "Go to the hotel. You need rest too. He's going to be sedated for a long time. He won't remember anything about tonight."

"Oh no," I said. "I've never done that before. I'll stay with him."

I knew the doctors were right: After such a long surgery, Nathaniel would most likely sleep through the night. But what if he woke up? Even though his eyes were sewn shut, I wanted him to "see" me and Russel right away. Ever since I'd kept vigil in a chair next to his bassinet in the NICU, I'd never left his side before or after a procedure, not even to get food while he slept. I barely went to the bathroom. And that's exactly what I planned to do now: Sit on the chair next to him, indefinitely.

Russel said, "She's going to be hard to convince."

But the doctors urged, "Trust us, it's going to be fine."

Russel and I went back in to say goodnight. Nathaniel was still resting comfortably.

So we went back to the hotel, had a bottle of wine, and watched *The Revenant* — that movie with Leonardo DiCaprio and the bear — to unwind. Some advice: *The Revenant* is a really bad movie for unwinding. Nonetheless, we fell asleep around midnight.

At 4:00 a.m. the phone rang, a startling interruption in the quiet night. A voice said, "We have an emergency, please come to the PICU *as soon as possible*. Nathaniel is flatlining." I was half asleep, but when I hung up I thought Nathaniel had died. For some reason I called my mother and told her that. I don't remember how Russel and I got to the hospital. All I know is that when I walked into the room, I saw right away that the monitors were on and he was stable.

Nathaniel had lost his heart rhythm for twenty-two awful seconds, but thanks to an amazing nurse and a few quick chest compressions, he had regained it quickly. The doctors reassured us that there was no loss of oxygen and no broken ribs, so there would be no long-term effects. They believed the incident was caused by a new sedation medication or an infection in his heart, but they couldn't be sure which.

Russel was thanking the nurses for saving Nathaniel's life, telling them how grateful we were for them, but I barely registered any of it. I was sitting on the floor, rocking back and forth, pulling my hair. It was the same surge of overwhelming shock that I had experienced when the doctor in North Carolina told me he had poked Nathaniel's brain (sorry, this is *really* the last time, I promise), the same intense distress that I was sure had given me cancer.

*Nathaniel: One of the medicines they gave me when I was asleep stopped my heart. Of course I had no idea this had happened, but a few days later, when I had my sight back and was able to write on my little tablet, I told my parents that I had dreamed I was in a blank room, and that our dog Coco was there, jumping on my chest and telling me to wake up. I didn't want to wake up because I was happy to see her and wanted to play with her.*

*My mom got a weird look on her face. Then she told me that I'd been clinically dead for twenty-two seconds and that the doctors had used chest compressions to bring me back to life. I had died and come back to life! Coco had helped! (Though the doctors and nurses also deserve some credit.)*

*We were all pretty blown away by that one. Coco had been gone for two years and was barely in my dreams anymore. We had two new dogs, Snowball and Brownie, in addition to*

*Smokey. But when I was dying, it felt like Coco had decided to help and comfort me.*

For three days after Nathaniel's heart had stopped, I sat next to him, staring at the monitors. I was afraid to leave, even just to go to the bathroom. Nathaniel was half sedated. His eyes were sewn shut — shifting his eyeballs or blinking would be too much movement for the delicate work they'd done near his eyes. His head was so swollen that we couldn't put his hearing aid back on. He was being fed through a g-tube. He says he really didn't like the part when he couldn't see or hear, which is his understated way of saying it was his darkest moment. With his eyes forcibly closed, it was literally dark.

Nathaniel doesn't talk much about pain. Like my dad, he has a remarkable ability to shift his focus from physical pain to other things. But he says the only thing that got him through those first couple days was having Russel sit very close to him, talking loud enough so he could hear, telling him every story he could think of about each of the dogs and trying to remember entertaining bits from the *Simpsons* episodes Nathaniel liked most.

After two days they took the sutures out of his eyes, but even so he couldn't see well because he was still swollen. Despite that, he never got scared. He never panicked. He handled it with incredible grace. Pain, hours of waiting, his body trying to rebound on so many fronts from the assault of the surgery. It was hard for him to entertain himself, and the only way he could communicate was to write, but even that was difficult. I had worked out an "I love you" signal in advance: three gentle squeezes of my hand. He did it over and over.

Little by little, as the swelling went down he could open one eye and try to watch a movie. Once both eyes were fully open, then he could communicate by writing, but even that was challenging. The first words he wrote in shaky, large letters on the LCD tablet we handed him were "no more drugs." He hated the jumbled feeling of the painkillers more than he minded the pain.

Six days after major craniofacial surgery that lasted eleven plus hours, Nathaniel was resting relatively comfortably in a room at the Ronald McDonald House, where he was supposed to stay for six weeks until the expansion of his facial structure was complete. Jacob was in Reno for lacrosse camp with Russel while Nathaniel recovered, and one weekend they came to visit. Jacob was really excited to see his brother, but when he came into Nathaniel's room, I saw a sad aura come over him. He wanted to talk and play, but Nathaniel couldn't do anything but play video games. Jacob kept him company while Russel and I went downstairs to prepare his food, and he told us later that as soon as we were gone, Nathaniel started crying. Jacob assumed it was because of the pain, but Nathaniel insists it was frustration. Since he couldn't talk, he wrote a note to Jacob on his little whiteboard that said, "Stop looking at me. I don't want you to see me like this."

A few days into his visit, Jacob was taking pride in helping his brother communicate. Nathaniel's mouth was wired shut, and Jacob was the best at understanding what he was saying. If Nathaniel said, "Hmm hmm hmm hmm hmmm hmm," I couldn't figure it out and would ask him to repeat it, but Jacob knew he was saying, "I need to go to the bathroom."

*Nathaniel: When I felt my worst, it was hard to believe this surgery was a good idea. I didn't even look forward to getting rid of the trach. Mostly I lay in bed, dreaming of eating pasta. One day I was sitting in bed in this near-constant state of*

*frustration when Jacob ran into my room, hit the wall above
my head, and ran out. Then he did it again.*

*I was a cannon, ready to explode. When Jacob hit the wall,
it was like the Fourth of July. With my mouth wired shut, I
couldn't yell at him to stop. I made a frustrated noise, stormed
downstairs, and ferociously typed on my iPad to tell my dad. I
know Jacob was behaving like a normal little brother, but if he
really cared about me, he wouldn't have the audacity to tease
me at my lowest point. He still thinks that how mad I got is
hysterically funny. I think he's half-jealous of the attention I
get. You'd think he'd be over that already. I keep trying to explain that I can do without the attention.*

*Every time I had a jaw distraction, there were screws that
needed to be tightened daily in order to slowly expand my
bones, but this time there were more than ever before. At the
Ronald McDonald House, when my parents first started turning the screws, I didn't feel it. But the more they twisted, the
more unpleasant it got, until it was an aching pain. After three
weeks, when the doctors thought they'd gone as far as possible, when I'd been stretched as far as a kid could possibly be
stretched, and the X rays confirmed it, we locked everything
in place.*

The expansion had taken less time than the doctors had anticipated. The device would stay on until the bone healed—four
months total—but the doctor told us, "Everything is good. He's
stable and you know what you're doing. You can go home for two
or three weeks until your next checkup."

We had our room at the Ronald McDonald House for a few
more weeks, but Nathaniel would thrive best at home, in his own
environment, with the dogs to comfort him. We knew how to take

care of him, even if it still didn't come to me easily. I remembered the first time I had tried to suction Nathaniel's trach—he gagged and I promptly threw up. I'd come a long way since then, but I would never be a natural nurse. Whenever Russel was around, Nathaniel would ask him to handle medical procedures. He'd say, "I love her, Dad, but you've got to do it. She's not gentle."

Russel and Jacob had already left. The day after the doctor set us free, I packed up the room, cleaned, and put everything in the car. Nathaniel and I set out early the next morning on the twelve-hour drive to Reno. Nathaniel was semi-reclined in the passenger seat, surrounded by pillows, and every three hours I stopped and fed him. In a strange regression, I was back to feeding him through a g-tube, and to feed him in the car, I sanitized my hands and the syringe with wipes and a bottle of water. It wasn't exactly a sterile environment to start with, and then it got worse.

I took a "short-cut" to avoid the main highway because I wanted privacy when we pulled over to feed him. The downside to this was that our route had very curvy roads. We were making good progress when Nathaniel tapped my arm and gestured wildly. I looked over and saw a panicked look in his eyes—his face was turning purple. He was throwing up, except his jaw was still wired shut! He was choking! Reaching over, I opened his trach (which would stay in place until he healed), and vomit came out through the hole.

I pulled over and suctioned the trach. Then I thought about how much trouble we'd be in if there was a real emergency. We'd driven for miles without passing a gas station and with no cell signal, and there was no sign of anything ahead. We had the privacy I'd wanted: There were no other cars on the road. But we were in the middle of nowhere, with no help if we needed it. I got us back on the road headed toward civilization as quickly as possible.

The roads were very dark as we drove through the desert out-side of Reno. We were on a divided highway when I noticed a car right next to mine, moving slowly with its hazards blinking. It was very strange. I was afraid it was a carjacker so I kept my eyes fo-cused straight ahead. A moment later, I almost hit a horse. When I stopped, I saw there were several horses running on the park-way. Drivers had turned on their hazards to alert others as Animal Control tried herding them off the road. I'd anticipated many ob-stacles before making this journey, but wild horses on the highway hadn't made the list.

*Nathaniel: My face was really swollen at first, a marshmallow face that I was afraid was going to be mine forever. Then the swelling went down and I didn't look much different.*

*My mom has always told me that when I was a baby, for-mula made me barf, so it was funny/not funny to discover that now, having a g-tube again at thirteen, I was able to con-firm her story. When I was in the Ronald McDonald House, they fed me formula and I felt nauseated all the time. It got better as soon as I was allowed regular food (that had been liquified).*

*While I was being fed, I played on my iPad. Being fed through a tube wasn't satisfying. Eating and getting full with-out ever tasting a bite is a really strange sensation, and when I was done, I still wanted to feel food in my mouth. It was like watching a movie without being able to hear anything. I could feel the temperature of the food. If it was really hot, I'd feel the warmth in my belly, but since it was summer I preferred cold foods. More than anything, I was dying for pasta. Mom made it for me, but of course I couldn't taste it. Spaghetti and meat-*

*balls through a tube that goes directly to your stomach just isn't the same.*

*Mom taught Jacob to feed me, for "emergencies" she said, but I'd rather have eaten a porcupine than let him do it. I wasn't letting him near a hole in my stomach for a lot of reasons. He may be good at lacrosse, but I wasn't confident in his g-tube technique.*

*When I felt my worst, it was hard to believe this surgery was a good idea.*

We questioned our decision each and every day. Life with a trach hadn't been so bad, had it? Why were we putting him through this? Were we the worst parents on the planet? Was this just too much?

Nathaniel had a problem with a tear duct in his right eye, which led to a series of complications. He went into the operating room for yet another surgery. While making one last trip to the bathroom, he decided it was the time to dance. On a blog for family and friends following Nathaniel's progress, Russel wrote:

*Wires, screws, g-tube, jaw wired shut, four pounds of metal strapped to his face and yet he danced! As if to say, "I got this, Daddy! Stop worrying!" He smiled through the bars and screw-turning and blood and wires and stitches and stares and pain and g-tube. He worried more about his momma than himself. He found ways to let his puppies lick his beaten face. He managed to tolerate Jacob. He let me kiss him. He laughed and danced and loved. He found ways to be the miracle that he is.*

• • •

Nathaniel: I've been in the hospital enough to know my way around. I don't worry—I just go with it. If I'm in pain, I don't ask for medicine. Instead, I think about something else until it goes away. If it gets really bad, I tell them that it kinda hurts, but on a pain scale of one to ten, the highest number I usually say is a three because I don't want them to drug me. The meds make me feel nauseated and droopy, which is worse than being in pain.

The only time I gave my pain a ten was when my IV shifted and the fluid was going into my skin instead of a vein. It happened in the middle of the night. My wrist swelled up. It felt better as soon as they took it out. They wanted to put a new one in, but my dad told them not to. He knew that all I wanted was to go back to sleep.

There were more complications with this surgery than I'd ever had before. I kept thinking I was about to feel better when another issue would come up. I'd get sick, or they'd decide I needed to fly to Seattle for another procedure. My face—the main focus of everything we were doing—was coming along great. But my stupid eye, which was supposed to be a minor side surgery, just kept causing problems. Everything that could go wrong did. That eye was so annoying—at some point I just wanted them to give up on it. They ended up doing seven procedures after the big surgery, and when I say "procedure," I mean I had to be put to sleep while they fixed something. Anyone else would call that a "surgery."

I wanted to go home. I wanted to see my puppies. I don't like being hooked up to things, and there were a million devices attached to me, beeping and whirring, measuring my heart rate and my oxygen level.

*One of my earliest roommates was a guy who was maybe in his twenties. I was awake, sitting in bed, doing nothing for hours at a time. All I heard was him cursing, moaning, and calling for his parents. I assumed from the drama on the other side of the room, that he'd been shot in the gut and both his legs had been simultaneously broken. It turned out he'd had toe surgery. Mom got us moved to another room.*

# 26. complicated complications

This time I just had a cough.

It was late May. Just four weeks earlier, Nathaniel had come home from Ronald McDonald House with the cumbersome cage on his head. He was finally stable enough that Russel felt confident flying across the country to start his new job.

I figured the cough was allergies, so I stopped by the doctor to get it checked out. He took an X ray and told me he saw a tumor in my lungs that looked cancerous, then promptly referred me to an oncologist. Ridiculous! I couldn't possibly have cancer again. I barely felt sick and figured all I needed was some nasal spray or an antihistamine.

Besides, I'd been through this cancer fake out thing before. The doctor who'd diagnosed my hip problems had also thought it was cancer at first, and I'd had a very similar cough eight months earlier. When they X-rayed my chest back then, I'd been diagnosed with walking pneumonia and whooping cough. And by the way, they told me, I had scar tissue from previous tumors in my lungs that could be mistaken for cancer. So I was pretty confident this doctor—a family practitioner—was wrong. I spoke to

Russel, who was in Connecticut. We agreed that the doctor had seen old scar tissue and Russel called him to cuss him out for scaring me needlessly.

A few hours later I started to get nervous. I called the doctor and begged for a CT scan so I could relax and get some sleep. He kindly let me come back that very night.

The next day, Nathaniel and I went to pick up Jacob from lacrosse. (I wasn't comfortable leaving Nathaniel alone, so I brought him with me, cage and all, when I had to go out.) The doctor called with the results of the scan while we were driving home. I was so certain there was nothing to worry about that I had him on speaker when he delivered the news that I had cancer. Again.

In the back seat, both kids immediately started crying. "Are you going to die?" they wanted to know.

"They still don't know what they're talking about," I told them. But a dark shadow of dread had already started to come over me.

The next day I called Dr. Newman (no relation), the oncologist who had saved my life in North Carolina.

"I'm coughing, and they think it's cancer," I told him. "Crazy, right? I've been in such good health. These people don't know what they're talking about. Would you mind if I had them send you the scan?"

Dr. Newman agreed. He would review it and call me back before I went to a local oncologist.

At the time, I'd been going through the process of becoming a US citizen. In fact, when I called Dr. Newman, I was on my way to an appointment at the immigration office. I was supposed to give my fingerprints and get my photo taken. Leaving Nathaniel at home, with Jacob to keep an eye on him, I drove to the same office I'd been to a couple times before. At the front door were three beefy guys working security.

"Please silence your phone before you enter the building," one said, and waited for me to do it. I had no idea how soon Dr. Newman would be calling me back, but I didn't intend to miss him. I looked around the foyer. There was nobody else there.

"I'm so sorry," I said, "but I'm waiting for a very important call. I'm about to find out if I have cancer."

"No." One of them blocked my passage. "Turn off your phone right now."

Maybe they thought I was joking. I didn't look sick. In fact, in my Lululemon sweatpants and sneakers, I was a picture of health. Not wanting to argue, I did as they said, near tears.

"If we see you talking on it," another guard added, "we'll escort you out of the building."

When I sat down in the waiting area, a woman sitting near me asked me a question about filling something out. As I helped her, tears sprang to my eyes and dripped onto her form.

She asked why I was crying, and gave me a hug. Receiving sympathy from this stranger made me start crying for real. I sobbed, "I'm scared because I'm about to find out if I'm sick." Then I saw Dr. Newman's name appear on my phone. I answered the call, beefy security guards be damned.

I knew from the tone of his voice that it wasn't good news. I started shaking. "Magda, I can't believe this is happening," he said. "I'm so sorry."

I started wailing; I've never been quiet when I get bad news. "Am I dying?" I asked.

"I hope not," he said, "but this is bad luck. You were about to be ten years cancer-free." Being in remission for ten years is a major milestone, marking the end of oncology visits and scans. Dr.

Newman continued, "The good news is that it looks like lymphoma." My cough had me worried that it was lung cancer; lymphoma was more treatable.

And that's how I found out I had cancer again: with strangers, in public, about to get my picture taken for my citizenship. An older man who worked in the office came over to me—my anguish had gotten everyone's attention—and as he did, I saw that the evil security guys were also approaching us.

"I'm sorry," I said, "I just found out I have cancer." Then I pointed down the hall at the advancing troops. "Those guys want to kick me out for using my phone. They think I'm lying."

He called his supervisor, who came out and called off the guards. I heard him say to them, "What were you thinking? You can't treat people like that." Then it was time to have my photo taken, in spite of the fact I was still crying.

"I look terrible," I said to the old man as I was leaving, laughing through my tears.

"If you hate it, come back," he said. "We'll do another." Then he walked me out of the building. As we passed security, he warned them, "You and me, we're gonna talk."

He escorted me all the way to my car. Sitting in the driver's seat, I called my mother and told her the news. Then I called Russel and said, "This is real. You have to come home."

It was day three of Russel's new job. I'd had a cough when he left for Connecticut, but the last thing that had been in either of our heads was the possibility that I had cancer again. I had been in remission for so long.

Russel called Brian, the friend who had been our salvation when he was unexpectedly fired. "You're not going to believe this," he said. "Magda was just diagnosed with cancer." He was afraid Brian would think that he had started work—three days earlier!

—knowing I was sick, angling for health benefits or something. Russel told Brian he should rescind the offer. We didn't know if or when he would be able to return to work.

Brian replied, "Listen to me, and listen good. Go home and take care of your wife, and as far as anyone else is concerned, you're here at work every day." Knowing my husband, I'm sure he wept in gratitude. It was only through the goodness of Brian's heart that Russel kept his job through everything that came next.

The day after Russel got back to Reno we went to a local specialist. She said, "You need to go to a top oncologist. I just don't have the resources here."

Russel looked at the diplomas on her walls. "You have an impressive resume. I'm sure you're capable of treating her. What are you doing in Reno?"

She smiled and said, "I have young children, and my family is here. I'm capable—" she looked at me "—but this looks like lymphoma, and because you've had cancer before, you need to be at a research hospital."

Russel thanked her for being honest and open with us, then I said, "I'm trying to get an appointment with a doctor, but he's too busy to see me. What should I do? Should I pack up and go without an appointment?" True to character, Russel had already been on the phone with Dr. McCarthy at NYU and Dr. Hopper at Seattle Children's, and they'd recommended Dr. Oliver Press at the Fred Hutchinson Cancer Research Center in Seattle, who was supposed to be one of the best lymphoma doctors in the country.

She replied, "If I were you, yes. I would go to the hospital and try to get in."

I bought a one-way ticket to Seattle, not knowing how long

I'd end up staying. First thing the next morning, I went to Fred Hutch and handed the folder with my medical history to a woman that Russel had spoken to. "I'm here," I said, "and I'm waiting for an appointment." I told her about Nathaniel's situation, unabashedly playing the pity card. Then I sat down and coughed in the lobby for an entire day. When the office closed, I went to the closest hotel, then returned the next morning to resume my vigil, staring at the receptionist with the pleading expression of my dogs watching me eat steak. Finally, she called me over. "Dr. Press will see you the day after tomorrow, first thing in the morning."

Two days later, I met with Dr. Oliver Press who, among many other accolades, was the acting director of the Clinical Research Division of the hospital. He was the best, and we had heard that he was no longer seeing patients. I gave him a grateful hug and said, "Who made this happen?"

He said, "Your son's doctor. He told me your story and I had to see you."

I didn't find out until later that he was struggling with his own cancer. That was why he wasn't seeing any more patients. He had already tried every drug, every trial, every option. At that point he was doing all right, but over the next month or two I would see his condition decline. I felt blessed to be in the skilled and caring hands of someone who was dying from the same disease.

Dr. Press said the fact that I had gotten a second, different type of lymphoma was a medical mystery. He theorized that my first diagnosis, nine years earlier, was off, and that my treatment had been missing one key drug. Regardless, we had to deal with the situation in front of us. This go-around would require very intense five-day rounds of chemotherapy in the hospital that I would receive every three weeks for four months. Five days of chemo every three weeks for four months: a protocol that was impossible to internalize. Thanks for nothing, chemo protocol creators.

God had brought me cancer twice. Was I cursed? I had worked so hard to become healthy and strong. We were hopeful that we were about to turn a corner with Nathaniel. He would gain freedom, and with it I, too, would achieve a new level of independence. This wasn't a minor obstacle on that path—it might well be the end of it. I felt envious of people who were healthy and had healthy children, people whose decisions revolved around whether their children had good teachers and where to go on vacation. I was jealous of the women around me, wives and mothers who built their dream homes and actually got to raise their families in them.

My mother, the devoted Catholic, had begged me to go to church to pray for my health, so I went the next time we were in Seattle. The first thing the priest said to the congregation was, in effect, "Let's blame Jews and Muslims for all the bad in the world. So many wars! Let's pray for them because they're stirring the pot." As I sat there listening, I wondered what good it did to spread anger at other religions. That was all I took away from that mass, and I never went back.

I couldn't say why this was my fate, but I refused to think that God was cruel. Instead, I chose to believe he had a plan. I believed my illness had been triggered by the stress of the night when Nathaniel flatlined, just as I believed that the stress surrounding his botched surgery had caused it nine years earlier.

The cancer was similar. The circumstances were similar. My prognosis was equally grim. But this time was different because I refused to believe I would die. I was as strong as I'd ever been, and I was ready to win.

After I filled Russel in on my meeting with Dr. Press, he told me a realtor would meet me in the lobby at lunchtime. Our days of commuting from Reno had to end. Now that half of our family was in treatment in Seattle, we needed to be there full-time.

Two years before Nathaniel's big surgery, when we were still meeting the doctors and they were examining him, Russel had taken him to a restaurant near Seattle Children's hospital. As they were eating, a woman approached them and said, "Hey, I just read a book called *Wonder* . . ." They struck up a conversation that culminated with her asking if Nathaniel could visit her son's third grade class to sign books. The next day, between appointments, Russel and Nathaniel went to the school and talked to the kids.

Two years later, on the day I was diagnosed, Russel dug up that woman's business card and called her. Ann was the only "friend" either of us had in Seattle — a woman he'd met over a milkshake at a burger joint. He asked if she could somehow help us find a place to live in Seattle. Immediately. Without hesitation, she connected Russel with a friend who was a realtor, and that woman canceled all her afternoon appointments in order to meet me and find us a new home. There are amazing people in the darkest moments.

I found a house that very day and signed a lease, and we told the children we were moving to Seattle, uprooting ten-year-old Jacob for the fifth time in his life and twelve-year-old Nathaniel for the seventh. Then we bought a second car from CarMax and stuffed everything we could fit into the two cars — including three dogs and Nathaniel with the cage around his head, needing to be fed every three hours through a tube — and moved ourselves to Seattle in time for my Monday morning biopsy. It was June 6th.

For anyone keeping count, that was seven weeks after we left the Ronald McDonald House, eleven weeks after Nathaniel's big surgery.

We put the house in Reno up for sale. I left it spotless, walking out backwards as I swept so there were no footprints.

## 27. muscle memory

The first time I got cancer, I went to a wig-maker in Charlotte who studied my face and coloring and then created a $250 custom wig for me from real hair, a horrible old-lady bob. Then I waited for my hair to start falling out.

This time I didn't hesitate. The day before my first round of chemo, I went to a hairdresser. I didn't tell her I had cancer. I just said, "I want to shave my head!"

Excited, she asked, "Have you ever done it before?"

"No!" I responded.

I ordered a few fun wigs from Amazon: a purple one, a short one, one with long blonde hair coming out from under a baseball cap. Cheap wigs made from fake hair, not high-quality expensive wigs of church-ready hair. That's how I went into cancer #2: like a purple-haired warrior.

Elizabeth Vargas told me that when I called to tell her I had cancer, she was sure we were pulling out of the show.

"Why would I do that?" I asked.

"You have so much stress right now," she said. "I thought maybe you'd decide this wasn't worth it. You're not getting paid and you're putting your life out there."

The truth is it never crossed my mind to quit 20/20. As upset as I was at the diagnosis, muscle memory immediately kicked in. I'd done cancer already; it was part of my journey. Our family was doing the show to draw attention to the craniofacial community, and the value of that hadn't changed, and besides, maybe the drama of my illness would make the show a little spicier.

Chemo was a dream. The first round required me to spend five days in the hospital. It was like being at a spa: I had a quiet room to myself with Wi-Fi, my iPad, and books. The first night, I got the best sleep I'd had in two months. They let me bring my resistance bands so I could exercise. I put some Les Mills on my iPad and quickly developed a routine with the bands. On my second day I offered to lead a workout for the entire oncology floor, but there were no takers.

I make it sound like a walk in the park, but Russel remembers that time a little differently. It must be part of my survival mechanism to block out my darker moments because when he reminds me of them, I say, "Oh, come on, it wasn't that bad." But I do remember thinking my life sucked, and seeing people living perfect lives all around me made me mad at everybody, even God. There were days when I wanted to die, when I screamed at Russel, "I hate you! I hate my life! I'd rather be dead." Most of the time I pushed my anger aside—who had time for such indulgences? —but it would build up, as these things do. By Russel's calculation, 85 percent of the time I smiled, danced, and loved my way through life, but the other 15 percent was scary enough that he hid the steak knives.

I never released my rage when I was with the kids, but eventually I would explode. When I was growing up, if my parents had something to say, they didn't fume silently; they went all out. If they had a disagreement, we all knew about it. Russel's parents aren't exactly quiet either. Some people see a therapist once a week to talk through their problems. I handle stressful times differently: I'm good for six weeks or so, then we'll get a huge medical bill or something else will go wrong and I have a moment. Then I'm good again. Venting helped, 100 percent — it was healthy for me, like a mental shower. Russel had his moments too, but he would sit and cry. I never cry. I scream.

I used Russel as a punching bag because he said I could, but also because it infuriated me that he had a life apart from the mess of our family. In the morning, he'd leave for the office, where he had his work and his friends, but I didn't have that option. Everywhere we'd lived, starting with Hal's basement, I was stuck, but Russel wasn't. Deep down, I hated him for having his independence and wished I could start over again in a life where I was healthy and perfect, and we lived in a house with a white picket fence.

My three youngest siblings, Michal, Eva, and Julia, traveled from Poland to Seattle to take care of Jacob, Nathaniel, and the dogs when I had to be in the hospital. Russel was mostly around, but he had already taken a lot of time off work and wanted to prove to Brian that keeping him on staff was the right thing to do.

I barely grew up with these three — Julia is twenty years younger than I! — but through the miracle of Skype we are very close. For the first year of Nathaniel's life, I was too busy and sad to talk to my mother, and she was very upset, so after that, we talked almost daily. She was a voice of reason for me. Eventually, I sent them a computer and a webcam.

The first time we talked using Skype, we went wild. I had a cup of coffee, my mother had a cup of coffee, and we were in our respective living rooms, giddy with joy that we could see each other across the ocean! Skyping with her became part of my daily routine. My mother was technologically useless, so my brothers and sisters had to help her get online every day. I'd ask them about their lives, and that is how I got to know them, seeing them every day on that screen.

I absolutely trusted my siblings not just to keep the household afloat, but to do things my way. Michal is a rock star. He knew how to handle the dogs because he had stayed with us in Reno to help out during Nathaniel's big surgery. Julia had also come for part of that and was very responsible (plus she loves to clean!), and Eva was in school studying to be a pharmacist, so she had some level of medical training. They learned how to feed Nathaniel through the g-tube and suction his trach. They bought fresh fruit and made sure Jacob ate. It comforted me to know that they were not only taking care of Nathaniel but also entertaining Jacob by shooting hoops with him in the driveway and learning how to play lacrosse. It was heartwarming that my boys were getting to know their aunts and uncle.

Every time Michal picked me up from the hospital, he'd take me to get a juicy burger, then we'd head home for a glass of wine. When I walked through the front door, everything was perfect. The house was clean, the laundry was done and put away, and Nathaniel, Jacob, and the dogs were happy.

## 28. a new face

On August 9, 2016, four months after Nathaniel's halo went on, it was ready to come off. This was another eleven-hour surgery that started at 8:15 in the morning. At the time, I was only halfway through my treatment, and the chemo had kicked in hard. My risk of infection was super high so the doctors didn't want me anywhere near the hospital, but I would not miss sending Nathaniel into surgery. He sat on my lap all morning. After Russel carried Nathaniel to the operating room, Michal drove me home, where I slept in my own bed instead of a chair in the hospital waiting room.

It was the end of the summer. My sisters had left, but Michal was staying for another month, sleeping on our living room couch. Pat Chibbaro, the nurse from NYU, had come in for the surgery, and she slept in Jacob's room. Jacob slept with Russel and me. Our house was often packed to the gills, but we always found a way to make it work.

Pat and I had formed a real friendship outside of the hospital. She radiates positive energy and immediately connects with people—it's her gift. Whenever I talk to Pat I know there's going to be laughter, even right before a scary surgery. With Pat, you'd be laughing on your deathbed.

For this procedure, Pat was in the OR watching out for Nathaniel and texting me and Russel updates. Removing the halo was the easy part. Using 3D imaging and modeling, templates and plastic "cutouts" were created prior to surgery to guide Dr. Hopper in shaping new cheek bones and eye sockets for Nathaniel. A neurosurgeon took two bone grafts from his skull to be used for the reconstruction. This was very important—Nathaniel's eyes would now be protected, and they'd be situated in the correct place relative to his new facial structure. It would also change his appearance, which made us a tiny bit sad: His perfectly imperfect face needed no changing; however, this adjustment was about the safety of his precious eyes.

Dr. Hopper then fit the grafts into place and adjusted as needed, then they were secured with small plates and tiny permanent screws. Over time, this would all fuse together and become one solid bone. Finally, Dr. Hopper moved Nathaniel's eyes forward to rest comfortably in his newly reconstructed face, a part of the operation that I understood was going to happen, but could never bring myself to picture.

Being at home, sick in bed, during this surgery felt like a failure. I was used to waiting with Russel, sleeping while he read, and feeding off of each other's love. I wanted to be there in the hospital, to protect my son.

We were optimistic that our ultimate goal, trach removal, was now in sight. To find out if Nathaniel could handle it, we needed to do a sleep study to track how often his breathing slowed or stopped during the night, but that wouldn't happen for another few months.

I was back in the recovery room by the time Nathaniel was brought out of surgery. To see his new face floored us—it was as if Dr. Hopper and his team had given him the face he was intended to have. Russel and I kept looking at Nathaniel, then at each other, then back at Nathaniel and each other again. We were filled with emotions: Did we miss his old face? Would he accept all of the changes?

Although Nathaniel was named after the mythical Scandinavian prince from my childhood books, Russel likes to say that he was named for his grandfather, Norman Koslow. Looking at our son's face, Russel saw his Popi. He turned to me and said, "Nathaniel is a Koslow through and through. A surgeon has restored my son to what God or nature intended all along."

*Nathaniel: When Dr. Hopper said the surgery would change my face, I said, "Okay, but not too much. I want my dogs to recognize me."*

*I was not in the best shape when I woke up. I thought getting the halo off would feel good, like pressure had been relieved, but in fact it felt like a knife had been ripped out of my head. My eyes were swollen shut again. Being blind for two days was scary and made me feel like I was going crazy. I don't think I was on pain medicine. I prefer to ignore the pain. This sounds heroic, but it's not that hard after surgery, which is like a planned, calculated injury. The element of surprise, like when you stub your toe, makes pain harder to handle because it comes out of nowhere, but I am pretty good at pushing it away when it emerges slowly.*

*In spite of the pain and swelling, my head felt much lighter without the halo — almost like I had super strength — and best of all, my jaws were free. The first meal I had was a big bowl of pasta and meatballs. It tasted soooo good — I'd been dreaming of that moment for so long. The doctors were right: I couldn't really chew, and I even had trouble swallowing. I think my muscles were really weak. But just being able to put food in my mouth and taste real flavors — that in itself was a huge improvement. For the first time in my life it made me happy to know that I'd be able to taste food every day. It felt like the best present I'd ever been given.*

## 29. two wonders meet

The producers of *Wonder* had invited us to visit the set in Vancouver, and we scheduled our trip for a week after Nathaniel's halo was removed. It was a two-and-a-half-hour drive from Seattle, and to my surprise, the set, which consisted of a cluster of trailers and a big building that we later learned was the sound stage, was kind of hidden in the center of town. Each trailer had an actor's name on it, and we were beyond thrilled when we were shown to one with Nathaniel's name on it! Inside R.J. had left us multiple editions of the book, in each of which she had written, "We are all wonders" above her signature.

We were escorted by Todd, the producer, to the soundstage. It was hot on the set, and as soon as they stopped filming, all the fans turned on at full speed, buzzing loudly. There was a flurry of activity as people started talking and allowing themselves to cough. Crew members ran to the actors to fix their hair and makeup, and then everything was quiet again as they resumed shooting, and nobody could leave.

We also toured the sets of some of the rooms that would appear in the movie: a classroom, the Pullmans' kitchen, Auggie's room. The garden outside of Auggie's Brooklyn brownstone looked so realistic. The wooden floor inside was worn, like it had really been lived in. Even the window sills were a bit dirty, just like you'd expect them to be in a city. The level of detail was mind-blowing.

That day, we watched the same scene being shot over and over again. It was fascinating to see how much work and time it took to get that one scene right, especially because each time they did it I thought, *That was perfect! Leave it!* And then they'd say, "take number 40" and try again.

Todd asked for our "notes" and although there was nothing significantly wrong, we gave him some feedback. For example, they had Auggie talking on the phone, so we told them that even with the hearing aid, that doesn't really work for Nathaniel. We also mentioned that we thought Auggie's eyes would look more realistic if they were a little droopier.

Jacob Tremblay was doing a great job, and I told him that I

liked how he didn't move his head much. He said he'd been worried about that stiffness, which was due to the prosthetic face being uncomfortable and restricting his movement. But because of his trach and hearing aid—so many attachments—Nathaniel always walked carefully. Jacob's performance was authentic. Both heads were fragile.

Todd introduced us to the rest of the cast too. I was pleasantly surprised by Owen Wilson, who played Auggie's father and is a real what-you-see-is-what-you-get kind of guy. He made jokes with the kids and high-fived them. When Jacob (my son, not the actor Jacob Tremblay) exclaimed, "You sound like Lightning McQueen!" he replied, "I *am* Lightning McQueen!" and made a *ka-chow* sound that we all recognized from the movie *Cars*. He told us that *Cars 3* would be coming out soon, and it was cool to hear that news straight from the mouth of one of the movie's stars.

Jacob also talked to Izabela Vidovic, who plays Auggie's sister Via, about what it's like to have a sibling like Nathaniel. He suggested she emphasize the part when she's slightly jealous of how Auggie gets more attention, but then devastated when he's hurt by a bully. I heard him say to her, "You gotta show how intense that is."

Perhaps naïvely, I'd expected to have a special connection with Julia Roberts. She was charming, kind, and thoughtful, even bringing my kids board games and gifts, but I'd expected more. Here she was, playing the mother of a child with Treacher Collins, and I *was* such a mother. Even more, at the time I was cancer-bald and Nathaniel was still swollen. In my fantasy, Julia Roberts said to me, "This is so hard. As a mother, I feel your pain," and maybe gave me a hug. But there was a wall between us—even when she shook my hand, there was no squeeze. No feeling of connection or trust.

Later, when I had time to mull it over, I understood. She may be extremely talented at playing a great, caring mom, but she is a professional actress and she was at work. I wasn't necessarily relevant to that. I noticed that she spent every break with her own children, so I could see the loving mom in her. Most likely, that was her priority, and bonding with me wasn't part of her process.

Todd brought us to the makeup trailer, where photos of Nathaniel hung on the wall. While we were there, a makeup artist showed us the elaborate process to create Auggie's face. Nathaniel had been very excited to see how they turned Jacob into Auggie and he wasn't disappointed. The transformation wasn't just a matter of skillfully applying some makeup: Strategic contouring couldn't come close to what was required. There was an entire fake head, with a wig that was attached to a mold of Jacob's face. An inch-high layer of goop was spread onto the mold and had to be redone every day. Hidden under the gooey material was a mechanism that ran from one eye down to his hand, where there was a button he pressed to make his eye droop whenever the camera was on. Jacob said it was really hot in the mask.

I couldn't help thinking of the irony: It must have been very expensive to make Jacob's prosthetic face. If the movie's producers had hired someone with Treacher Collins, they could have used all that money to pay for surgery on the faces of twenty kids who needed help. If you look at it as "face-changing money," was this the best way to spend it? When Russel and I discussed it, I told him I didn't think this would go over well in the community; there was already online buzz on the topic. But then we considered that raising awareness about kids with facial differences was the more valuable investment. How to achieve that was best left to the pros. Besides, it was difficult to imagine anything surpassing the authenticity Jacob Tremblay achieved as Auggie, even wearing that uncomfortable mask.

We were all getting tired so we headed back to our hotel. The next morning we had breakfast with the whole cast. All the kids, even if they weren't shooting that day, showed up to meet Nathaniel. Then we hurried back to Seattle because I had to be at the hospital for chemo at 2:00. My Hollywood life.

*Nathaniel: When I first talked to Jacob Tremblay, he had the Auggie Pullman mask on. It was strange talking to a kid who didn't have Treacher Collins but looked exactly like he did, but I almost forgot it was a mask because the way someone looks isn't a big deal to me. Well, it wasn't a big deal until they took it off: It looked like they were pulling his actual face off! Yeah, it was creepy, but boy would it have been more convenient to be able to peel off my face and call it a day than endure six months of surgeries, screws, and being in a cage.*

*We were on set for eight hours. After seeing how little of the story they shot in that time, I don't even know what anyone was thinking when they had me audition for Auggie! There's no way I could have spent day after day going slowly through the scenes; I would have lost my mind. It made me appreciate movies much more. The Wonder movie is only an hour and a half, but making it took months. What I learned from meeting Jacob was that it's not as easy as people think. Now if I don't like a movie, I'm inclined to blame the script. Those actors are endurance athletes!*

# 30. made whole again

Before Nathaniel got his trach out, there was a less significant port to have removed: mine. It connected a catheter to a vein so they didn't have to poke me with a needle to insert an IV every time they gave me chemo. The first time I had cancer, when I finished chemo, I drove myself to the appointment to get the port removed because Russel was traveling and my mother-in-law was taking care of the kids. Since I didn't have the luxury of an escort and would be driving myself home, the doctor couldn't give me any sedatives. Sitting on the table, I watched as he gave me a local anesthetic, then chatted with him as he took out a scalpel. I winced, but kept talking, when I saw how long the tube he pulled out of me was. It was not a pleasant sensation, but I got strength from knowing that I'd soon be going home to my kids. When the doctor was finished, I waited for about an hour to make sure there were no blood clots, then I drove home.

I planned on doing the same thing this time around. A couple weeks before Thanksgiving, I drove myself to the hospital. When I checked in, they asked me who was driving me home. I lied and said my father was waiting for me downstairs. When they were about to put me under, I told them it was unnecessary. "I can just watch," I said. "My doctor let me stay awake last time."

This doctor wouldn't allow it. "This is a surgical procedure. We're going to give you a sedative."

When I woke up, the nurse told me to call my father.

"Oh, that's okay," I said. "He's meeting me downstairs."

"I have to physically see him," she insisted. "He has to sign the release form."

I dialed my own cell phone number and pretended to have a

conversation with my dad, who was definitely not downstairs, or even in the country. He was probably watering tomatoes in Sanok. Then I told the busy signal at the other end of the line to call me back because I was ready to go and to give my mother my love, before walking back to the nurses' station, where they were eating lunch. "My father is on a walk," I said. "Please enjoy your lunch. I'll go meet him and bring him up here to sign me out."

Then I went downstairs and drove myself home, feeling guilty and a little proud.

Our Thanksgiving tradition was to deep-fry a turkey. In North Carolina, that's how all of our neighbors had cooked theirs. I'd had my doubts, so one year I roasted one bird in the oven while Russel fried another in peanut oil. We had a lot of guests that year, and when dinner was over, the deep-fried turkey was picked clean and my roast turkey was basically untouched. We never looked back.

This was our first Thanksgiving in Seattle. It was raining, of course. Russel put a tarp over part of the backyard to shelter the deep fryer while the rest of us, including my parents, who were visiting from Poland, sat on the porch. Jacob made all the side dishes, and I was his sous chef. It was still hard for Nathaniel to chew, so we cut up tiny pieces of turkey and mixed them into the mashed potatoes. Normally, Nathaniel doesn't like to eat food his brother made. He says he doesn't want to give his brother the satisfaction of having fed the family, but that Thanksgiving was the first time he didn't refuse to eat food Jacob had prepared.

Every year we like to go around the table and say what we're thankful for. This year it was a no-brainer. Every person at the table gave some form of thanks for everyone's good health. On previous Thanksgivings, we'd turned our attention outward, but this year we'd all had to be focused inward. I told my family I hoped we could put all our worries behind us and look forward to a future without any drama.

The next day, Jacob and I drove a mile up the street to where a guy was selling Christmas trees on a corner. Being native to the Pacific Northwest, these trees were thick and full, like in a storybook, and they smelled delicious. The boys love decorating the tree, though we call it a "Hannumas tree," and adorn it with blue ornaments, one shaped like a little menorah, and a sign that says "Happy Hanukkah." We have a video of Nathaniel from that year, standing in front of the tree and belting out the Miley Cyrus song "Wrecking Ball" with my dad in the background, cleaning wax off the menorah for Hanukkah, which would begin on Christmas Eve that year. After all we'd been through, we were all home together, healthy and full of joy.

Finally, in late January, the time came to remove Nathaniel's trach. We'd done a sleep study and Nathaniel was able to sleep with it fully capped, his breath silent and sure. This confirmed that he could breathe without the trach. It was a miracle—here was child who had been born with *no nasal airway*. Sixty-plus surgeries and procedures later, and at night he was now so quiet that it made me nervous—I was used to monitoring his breath, even in my sleep.

When parents first bring home a newborn, there's usually a moment when they stare at the crib, watching their sleeping baby's chest rise and fall peacefully. That night had eluded us for so long. Now it was ours.

"It's going to be so anticlimactic," Russel said the night before it was scheduled to come out. "Remove a few Velcro straps, slide out the trach, and slap on a Band-Aid. Then we'll walk out of the hospital and be on our merry way. It's too easy! After thirteen years with a tracheostomy, thirteen years with a hole in his neck, thirteen years of 'What's that in his throat—'"

I chimed in, "Thirteen years of infections, thirteen years of suctioning, thirteen years of cleaning, thirteen years in a tub instead of a shower—"

And Nathaniel added, "Thirteen years of 'Don't go underwater like all the other kids,' thirteen years of nurses—"

The family put it all out on the table: Thirteen years of challenges at school; thirteen years worried about a fall, a slip, a hit to the neck; thirteen years of checking oxygen levels; thirteen years of annoying calls with medical supply companies; thirteen years of meddling respiratory therapists; and, finally, thirteen years of questions about the future.

Russel exclaimed, "Thirteen years and I want marching bands! I want glitter falling from the sky!"

Then Nathaniel said, "Thirteen years and I'd like to know if I can bring my iPad and DS so I can watch movies and play games while they're working on me."

We all laughed.

Strangely, unexpectedly, Russel felt a little sad. He said it was because we'd spent so many precious moments with Nathaniel at night: Listening for his breath. Gently cleaning his trach. Making sure it was straight. Is the Velcro strap too tight or not tight enough? What's that smell? Is it infected? Suction? No suction?

Russel said to Nathaniel, "Promise me something. Promise I can always take care of you? Promise you will still need me?"

His response was classic Nathaniel. "Dad, I want my trach out. I never said I wanted them to take my Treacher Collins away. I'll always need you and Momma." Then he smiled and ran off to play Pokémon as if to, say once again, *Stop making it a big deal, Dad. I got this.*

*Nathaniel: Ten months had passed since the surgery, and ever since they'd taken off the halo I'd been practicing breathing through my nose and sleeping with the trach capped. Even with the trach closed, my oxygen level never dropped below 97 percent, which meant I didn't need it anymore. If you made a pie chart of how I spent my waking hours during my whole life, "dealing with the trach" probably ranked first, although "being annoyed by Jacob" or "hugging my dogs" were both close in the running. I mean, if I'd spent as much time playing the piano as I had in hospitals trying to get rid of the trach, I probably could have been a concert pianist like my mother. But for this, I wouldn't get a grade or receive a trophy for my efforts. I had to take everyone's word for it that my life would change for the better.*

*A crowd gathered around my hospital bed. It was Mom, Dad, Jacob, Dr. Johnson, and the camera guy from 20/20. It was kind of an intense moment, and it was also kind of a nothing moment. They took the trach out, something that we'd done every two weeks for my whole life, but this time, instead of putting a new one in, they just bandaged the hole and threw the trach in the garbage. Just like that.*

*After they took it out, we sat for a few minutes and talked. It felt so weird, like something was missing. Using my nose to breathe wasn't instinctive yet. If I stopped paying attention, I'd go back to breathing through my mouth, and then it felt like my trach had come out and I couldn't get enough air without it. I was scared of losing my breath, and worried that without my trach I'd suffocate. I didn't like that feeling.*

*Suddenly, it occurred to me that maybe I'd never get used to being without it. I'd had a trach my whole life. It had always been a part of my body; I never knew a time when it wasn't there. It was how I breathed. I couldn't grasp that I was going to live this way forever. It felt like a loss. Before I'd had three ways of breathing: through my nose, my mouth, and my trach. Now I only had two, like everyone else. How would I feel comfortable eating and sleeping without an open trach?*

*Quietly, I asked my mom to send everyone out of the room. When they were gone, and it was just Mom and me, I said what was on my mind.*

*I want my trach back. Can they put it back in?*

*Mom said, "Let's just wait an hour and see what happens."*

*I knew, obviously, that this was the whole reason I'd had the surgery and that horrible heavy halo. This was what my parents and all the doctors wanted for me. They had all worked really hard toward this for a long time. We'd all talked about how excited we were, and I was embarrassed to feel the way I did, but my trach was my security blanket. It always had a name. It changed over time, but the most recent one I'd had was named Charlie Hudson. It was hard to let Charlie go.*

The trach just popped right out. This was why we'd had to be so careful with it—because it came out easily, and the minute it did, his body would start healing itself. This was precisely what

I had fought *against* for so many years, so it felt really strange to actually want the trach to come out and the healing to begin. As Russel had predicted, the exact moment they removed it was . . . just a moment. Then they taped up the hole and it was done. Later that night, talking to Russel, I said, "All the suffering and hard work all came down to a single moment, that moment the trach came out. We succeeded. It was all worth it."

Dr. Hopper hadn't waved a magic wand over Nathaniel and gotten perfect results. This surgery was a new procedure and the doctors still had a lot to learn. Nathaniel's body rejected some of the plates that had been put in his head and one of the implants surrounding his eye. The wound on his head didn't heal quickly. He needed to have twelve follow-up surgical procedures that Izzy, the child who'd had the same surgery before him, hadn't needed. There were weeks when we'd rushed to the hospital five times. He was on antibiotics for three months after his heart stopped, in case it was an infection, and we added an infectious disease doctor to his team—but we finally reached the goal we'd worked toward his entire life.

Nathaniel is finally normal, and by "normal" I don't mean "like everyone else." I mean "free." For us, normal is an absence of need, an absence of special attention, an absence of fragility. He still has differences, but I don't care that he doesn't look like everyone else or still has a hearing aid. To us, his appearance was never a problem. It was the trach that caused the most illness, interventions, and stress. It was what kept him the furthest from normal.

I was almost normal too. I was done with chemo and my hair was growing back in. I hadn't gotten official word that I was cancer-free, but I knew in my head and my heart that I was fine. If my cancers had been reactions to Nathaniel's worst moments—getting his brain poked by a doctor, flatlining after this surgery—then my healing would follow his. Now we were both better; a double celebration.

It wasn't just Nathaniel who had stepped into the realm of normal. It was all of us.

## 31. gift from god

We called Nathaniel's thirteenth birthday party the "Ding Dong My Trach Is Gone" party. We hadn't been in Seattle long enough to make a lot of friends, but we invited the two boys who had showed Nathaniel around his new school. Hunter, a friend of Nathaniel's from Reno, came to stay for the week. The Tremblay family—Jacob, his sister, Erica, and his parents—also came. We invited Ann, the woman Russel had met in a burger joint, and her husband and children, as well as our realtor, Jen, and her two boys. Jacob invited the first friend that he made in Seattle, a classmate named JP.

The adults drank wine while the kids played with Nerf guns. Then a video game truck Nathaniel had requested arrived, and the kids disappeared into it until it was time for cake. Nathaniel ordinarily didn't like having "Happy Birthday" sung to him, but that year he didn't mind.

Thirteen is a milestone birthday, and I've always loved checking off milestones. Nathaniel had been through more of them than most children his age, but now he was in a game truck with the rest of them, thinking only about whether he was dominating Mario Kart.

• • •

The 20/20 cameras had been with us on and off during the period leading up to Nathaniel's big surgery, afterward, and throughout my cancer treatment. Now Nathaniel and I were in the home stretch of our medical issues, the *Wonder* movie would soon be released, and they were nearly done filming us. The producers wanted Elizabeth Vargas to do one final set of interviews, and for some reason they wanted to tape them in LA. We agreed, and when I texted Todd, *Wonder*'s producer, to tell him we were coming to town, he said, "If you stay an extra day, I can get you three tickets to the *Beauty and the Beast* premiere!"

We spent our first day in LA talking to Elizabeth at a home in the low hills that cradle the city. The crew told us they had rented that house on Airbnb, but we'd be going to a second location for the afternoon. They wanted footage of Nathaniel and Elizabeth walking with the sunset in the background. Going somewhere else just for a sunset sounded a little excessive, but whatever; I trusted they knew what they were doing.

Later that day, they loaded us into SUVs. A camera crew filmed us on the drive to the second location. This was also odd—why did they want footage of us driving?—but we figured this was their last chance to make sure they had everything they needed. We arrived at a neighborhood with armed guards at the gates. Strange. Then we pulled up to a gorgeous house.

The producers said, "We're going to film you here, but don't get out of the car yet. We want Elizabeth to greet you and walk you inside."

By now it was clear there was something they weren't telling us. I looked at Russel. He shrugged and mouthed "TV" as we walked toward the house.

Elizabeth opened the front door and welcomed us, which

seemed weird because we'd seen her literally five minutes before. Showing us inside, she said, "It's been so wonderful working on your story that we wanted to give something back to you."

Then Christina Aguilera walked into the room. We were in her house, and it was the nicest one I'd ever seen. She led us to her living room, which had a fireplace, sofas covered with white furs, gold décor, and a grand piano. She already knew our whole story. She'd read letters that Russel had written Nathaniel on every birthday, and she knew all about of the night of his birth.

After we'd talked for a while, she asked, "Would you mind if I sang 'Beautiful' to Nathaniel?"

Would we mind?

Then we sat five feet away from Christina Aguilera, in her living room, as she sang to us. She was tiny in person, but her voice was powerful. It gave me goosebumps. I thought, *This is the instrument we all have, but not all of us can use it.*

Her accompanist was playing on a shiny black piano with clean, classic lines in that grand room. Looking at it, I thought back to the antique instrument I'd learned on at my great-aunt's humble home. It was ornate, with carved legs and other decorative details; even the music stand had flowers carved into it. The music I played on that piano and afterward was classical, a very different genre. I grew up strictly following sheet music, adhering exactly to the instructions given by the composer. When Christina sang, she had a freedom of performance that I had never experienced. It was as if she and the pianist were having a conversation. They were looking at and supporting each other, and it was like he was talking with his hands. When you perform Bach, it's meant to sound the same every time. He tells you when to be loud or soft, fast or slow. When Christina sings, there is improvisation and inspiration that makes each performance unique.

Giving birth to Nathaniel took me off the sheet music. All the parents I knew read *What to Expect the First Year*. However, the day I brought Nathaniel home from the hospital, I threw mine out, both the Polish *and* English versions. There was no way to apply it to raising Nathaniel—I had to improvise every day. It was a different kind of music.

As Christina sang, Nathaniel held the Grammy she'd won for that very song, and Russel and I were transported back to the moment we had accepted Nathaniel as a gift from God. And this moment, in the present, was itself another gift from God.

As we walked out of Christina Aguilera's house, Russel said to Nathaniel, "Dude, what do you think? That was insane!"

Nathaniel asked, "What did I do to deserve this?"

Russel said, "The fact that you asked that question is exactly why you deserve it. You don't even realize."

Nathaniel doesn't see himself as a kid who's been through that much, and he accepts what he's had to endure. This makes us feel like he deserves everything good that comes to him. But he's right in that he isn't the only kid who's been through a lot. There is no way to even out the gifts and struggles we are handed, but we hope his life impacts the world for good.

The next day, we dressed up nicely for the *Beauty and the Beast* premiere, which was a matinée. We took photos with the boys, feeling very Hollywood, then left Russel behind at the hotel because we only had three tickets. We sat with Todd's family during the film, dazzled by every frame and how special it was to be among the first to see it.

John Legend and Chrissy Teigen were sitting right behind us. A celebrity is as much a magnet for undesired attention as a kid with a craniofacial difference; but nonetheless, I decided to approach the singer directly. "I hope you don't mind me coming up to you," I said, "but we want to tell you that my husband admires your music. Every time he's grilling dinner he puts on your songs." His reply was very gracious. His wife was dressed like a princess, and when she looked at Nathaniel, I noticed a millisecond of shock register on her face. I could tell she felt bad for her reaction, but I understood it so I tried to make her feel comfortable. Otherwise, I didn't focus on the rich and famous all around us. I just wanted my kids to have the most fun they could have without getting lost in the crowd.

But, for all the glitz, glamour, tears, and miracles, the best moment of our trip was when we took the kids to the Santa Monica pier. We rented bikes and rode along the beach. The boys were all big smiles. I felt the wind in my hair, the ocean breeze on my skin, and the warmth from the sun on my head. Nobody passing by would know what a crazy journey we'd had or how special it was for us to be traveling together just for pleasure, not to see more doctors. We looked like a regular family of four, enjoying a relaxing vacation—a normal thing that normal families do. We all had scars, but this was as close to normal as we got, and it was good enough for me.

## 32. a new normal

*Nathaniel: I went back to school in March. I'd done most of sixth grade in Reno, so in Seattle I was the new kid, showing up post-surgery, finishing out seventh grade with a bunch of strangers. I'd wanted to be homeschooled, but my parents said no.*

This time Dad and I didn't write a letter to prepare my classmates. Wonder had done that work for us. And, as seventh graders, we figured they should be able to handle me, and we were right.

Even so, on the first day I felt like I had walked into a movie theater when the movie was already nearly over. I was clueless in all my classes. There was no real recess where I could make friends. If they finished lunch early, some kids hung out on the basketball court, but that wasn't my thing, so I went to the library to read or do homework.

For the first time in my life, I didn't have a nurse shadowing me. It was only when I stopped having one that I discovered what it was like to be independent. I was so used to being followed. The nurses were okay, but it was never part of their job description that they had to talk to me or be fun. Mostly they were one more way in which I was a little bit different.

After a few weeks, things got better. In Language Arts I sat next to a kid, just chilling since I still didn't have friends. He was wearing a Pokémon shirt so we got into a conversation about that. Then I think he wanted to get at the fact that I have Treacher Collins but didn't know how to bring it up, so he said, "I'm Andy. I have Asperger's." I think that was Andy's way of saying that he was different too. We had that in common.

"Cool," I said. Then we started talking about random stuff like Minecraft and, just like that, Andy became my best buddy. From there, I started knowing my way around the school, I (mostly) caught up on schoolwork, and I spent hours after school with Andy playing video games and inventing superhero fantasies.

Andy has a cat named Bella who isn't very nice — she even

*gave Andy an exclamation mark–shaped scar—but Andy loves this mean cat. Once his grandparents came to visit him and brought their blind, deaf dog, who was also losing his sense of smell. If a dog can't smell, hear, or see, it can't do anything, so getting around the house was impossible for him. As the dog stumbled around, Bella kept pouncing on him. He was tiny, smaller than Bella, and he was terrified when he lost his balance. I felt so bad for him. It took a minute for me to connect his state to how I was during the big surgery. It was a sorry state, but I never thought of myself as pitiful. Maybe that old dog didn't either.*

*The end of the school year couldn't come quickly enough, and then it was summer. Summers had never been fun for me, but that summer, being trach-free opened up the world more than I expected. For instance, being in a windy situation had always been unpleasant before. One time, at a playground with my cousin Hayden, the wind rushed into the trach, overloading it with so much air that I couldn't breathe. But if I closed the trach, I'd have to breathe harder to get enough oxygen. Before surgery, I'd never sat around moping over the wind and its effects. I never thought,* Hey, I should go through surgery to change to shape of my face so that I can hang out on a windy day. *But now that I could, it was a nice improvement.*

*The best change came the first time I beat Jacob in a boxing match. We like to box on our trampoline, but since it would have been bad if he punched me in the trach, he was never allowed to hit me above my shoulders. That made it kind of boring, plus I couldn't win because he easily blocked my punches. I'd only ever won once before, on a glorious wet, slippery day. But this time, I somehow made him slip and trip, and there was no way he could claim that his ability to fight had*

*been restricted. At the time, he admitted I won, though later*
*he said that he let me win. I just said, "That's right kid." I'm*
*pretty sure I will win our next match too.*

  *I swam all that summer, sometimes at Beaver Lake and some-*
*times at my cousin's pool. At the pool, I liked to go down to the*
*bottom of the deep end and push off. It was exciting to be wear-*
*ing my goggles and holding my breath — my normal breath,*
*the air that came in through my nose — then going under-*
*water for as long as I wanted. My life didn't change when I got*
*rid of the trach; I was still me. I guess you could say it was kind*
*of like having a broken leg your whole life and then finally get-*
*ting the cast off.*

Nathaniel is blasé about the changes in his life, but, as his mother, life changed dramatically the day his trach went away. After thirteen years, I no longer had to do all the things that were required to take care of this foreign part of his body. We had a closet full of supplies that I would never need again. I donated some of the sealed boxes to myFace, hoping there wasn't a squad of cockroaches hiding within.

This feels strange to admit, but on the top shelf of the laundry room, where nobody goes but me, I still have a bag containing the stuff he needed to have at school: the ambu bag, containers for the suction pump, suction catheters, a hose for the pump, a spare trach, and antibacterial soap. The ambu bag, which was so critical, is now getting dusty on the shelf. It doesn't make sense to keep these things, especially now that they can't even be attached to Nathaniel, but I can't seem to let them go. They were my lifelines for so long, and deep down I guess it's hard to accept that I'll never need them again.

Another way in which our lives changed was that Nathaniel

could now shower on his own. That hadn't been an option with the trach, and I'd wondered what we'd do when he was at the age when he'd want privacy. (What teenager would want to shower with his mom helping him?) Now I no longer had to be there for him. I could wash dishes or drink a cup of tea while he was showering. It was another milestone to check off the list.

At thirteen years old, he had to learn how to wash his own hair. Before he went into the bathroom, I instructed, "Pour some shampoo into your hand, massage it into your hair and scalp, then rinse." At first he wasn't used to giving the top of his head a good scrub—I'd always had to be gentle, washing his hair section by section, moving very slowly so the water didn't drip into the trach. Letting go of worrying about the shower was difficult for me, even though there was literally nothing bad that could happen. Still, I couldn't kick the habit of knocking on the door to ask if he was okay.

Life with a hole in your neck is dangerous. All I ever wanted was for my children to be safe. The effort required to keep him safe on a daily basis was constant. Now he is as safe as anyone else.

We allowed Nathaniel to do "risky" things like playing at the playground, going to the beach, and riding a bike, never forgetting that his first craniofacial surgeon, Dr. McCarthy, had told us to make his childhood as normal as possible. Not a single bone was ever broken, and he had the biggest life he could within his constraints. I was happy that he was alive, and that the trach helped him live. But I was happier without the extra worries and stress.

Nathaniel started eighth grade after his first summer of "freedom." Jacob was starting sixth so they were both in middle school, the first time they had been in the same school in a while. Jacob, now my eyes and ears, came home and said, "Mom, Nathaniel's been chewing on his sleeve. Can you tell him not to do it?" Or "I saw him at lunch. He looks like a slob." Although he would never judge a kid who was different, Jacob wants Nathaniel to fit in as best he can, to be "cool." Nathaniel, on the other hand, doesn't care. He's a minimalist, which is a nice word for lazy. He still won't tie his shoes because it's too much work—he's literally been wearing Crocs and socks for about six years. I bought him $85 Timberland boots that Jacob was coveting, but he won't wear them because you have to tie them.

Nathaniel said, "You're trying to make me look cool, Mom. I don't want to look cool. I'm fine with whatever I'm wearing. I don't need clothes to feel better about myself." That was his excuse. Even if the real reason was pure laziness, it was hard to argue with that.

Jacob chimed in. "Nobody wears Crocs anymore. You're in eighth grade."

But Nathaniel said, "I don't care, Jacob. Mind your own beeswax."

For Halloween that year, Nathaniel was Vegeta, a character from the Dragon Ball manga series. He went to school in costume. Jacob reported that most of the eighth graders chose not to join the Halloween parade in the gym, during which everyone had a chance to take a solo moment up on the stage, or they ran on stage and then quickly ran off. But Nathaniel took his turn cheering, dancing, and hamming it up. No one else had the guts to go all out, but Nathaniel didn't care what anyone thought, and you could tell everyone was happy for him. Jacob told us his brother was smiling ear to ear.

I thought back to all the school plays Nathaniel had been in and how happy he was to be on stage. He had played the troll in "The Billy Goats Gruff" and a bully in another performance. In choir concerts he liked being front and center. I guess he inherited the pleasure I get in being seen and heard.

That October, when my parents came to visit, I took them to see the Grand Canyon. Jacob came too, but we didn't want Nathaniel to miss any more school, so Russel stayed with him. We also stopped in Las Vegas, where I surprised them with tickets to see David Copperfield. In Poland, we had watched his shows on TV with great amazement, so my parents were delighted.

We sat right by the stage. Just as the show was about to start, a side door opened and a woman came over to us with champagne in flutes and chocolate-covered strawberries. There was a note on the tray from Russel. It said, "Magda, you are cancer-free. The doctors just called and your scans came back clean."

Everyone in the theater could see us receiving this hand-delivered treat. For my parents, who are from such a small town in Poland, being the center of attention for a moment was a spectacular, over-the-top way for them to receive the best news imaginable. They blushed, uncomfortable but happy. I'm sure they'll never forget it—I know I won't.

## 33. the "real" *wonder* boy

A month after that trip, Russel, the boys, and I returned to LA for the *Wonder* premiere. 20/20 wanted to film us arriving on the red carpet—a happy ending where all happy endings are made —in Hollywood. But just before it was time for us to leave, I started feeling guilty. We had gotten to film the 20/20 feature, and we'd been on the set of the movie. I felt privileged and honored to be included in this too, but I said to Russel, "There are other kids with Treacher Collins who would love to have this experience. I want them to have a chance too." It was the same thing I'd asked Todd when they were looking for an actor to play Auggie: "Did you interview other children too?" My son isn't more special than the other kids—except to me, of course. I worried that people would think, *What did this kid do to be treated like royalty? Why can't we go?* Lots of moms in my position also have stories to tell.

Russel said, "There's no way to include everyone so just be humble and let Nathaniel have this. It's the only upside to all he's been through. Let's just be grateful." So I tried, and later I would be happy and relieved to see that other kids with craniofacial differences had been invited to and attended the premiere.

*Nathaniel: We got to ride in a limo to the movie theater, which was cool, and when we got out of the car we were on the red carpet, except it was white, and there were tons of photographers shouting, "Nathaniel! Over here! Over here!" to get me to look at their cameras. I was in shock. How did so many people know my name? There were lots of flashing lights.*

It's a Hollywood mystery as to how they did it, but it had clearly been choreographed, probably by 20/20, that we were first to arrive at the premiere. We were in a big Escalade with tinted windows. They stopped the car, and the 20/20 cameraman hopped out and ran ahead to get ready. The doors opened, and Nathaniel stepped out onto the carpet. For the next twenty minutes, the media went nuts. For the first three, Russel was hiding off-camera, sobbing. My heart was beating fast, not with nervousness, but with excitement.

Russel composed himself and we posed, documenting for posterity the brief but enormously popular dabbing trend.

•  •  •

When Nathaniel was born, I'd thought it was the end of the world. On our walks, I threw a blanket over his stroller so as not to draw attention. Now, at a moment when I was standing proud, he was too, announcing, *Look at me, people. I made it. I'm not embarrassed by who I am.* For him, this moment in the spotlight meant something different than it would to a "normal" kid. Everyone was looking at him, but they weren't staring. They wanted his picture because they appreciated how he looked for the courage it represented. It was an awesome moment.

We took our seats and the movie started. As soon as the first image appeared on the screen, Russel started crying again, and he didn't stop until the screen went dark. Nathaniel whispered that he wished it could go on forever. The hardest part for me was when Via, Auggie's sister, said, "August is the Sun. Me and Mom and Dad are planets orbiting the Sun." I looked over at Jacob and he was crying, just like his dad. Later, he said that it reminded him of how badly Nathaniel used to be treated. He said it hadn't been as extreme as in the movie—nobody ever told Nathaniel that he should kill himself, or drew pictures saying he looked like Freddy Krueger—and what the real-life kids did hadn't really fazed Nathaniel. But Jacob had noticed how much the unpleasant looks and rude comments decreased when the book came out. He said, as he had before, "I think *Wonder* helped me more than it helped Nathaniel."

*Wonder* is a warm, feel-good family movie, and Jacob Tremblay brought Auggie to life. When I walked out of the theater, I felt like there was good in the world. *Good* triumphs. And *Wonder,* the book and the movie, in real life, in our lives, is helping good to win. This was Hollywood, but it was real.

When the movie came out, however, as we'd predicted, there

was a small whisper of protest from the craniofacial community because they hadn't cast a boy with Treacher Collins. Most people admitted that Jacob was amazing in the role, but then they might add, "He didn't look severe enough. He should be drooling more." A film critic even discussed that it was ironic that the movie was championing the community, but someone with a craniofacial difference wasn't good enough to act in it.

Russel and I just shook our heads. *Wonder* was a blockbuster and the value of the awareness it generated for Treacher Collins is immeasurable. The movie was made for a young audience, and the producers wanted it to reach broadly. We knew from experience—the very experience that had inspired R.J.—that facing people with differences didn't come naturally to young children. It made sense to ease children into it.

But millions of people loved the movie, and there were so many others in the craniofacial community who focused on all the good that came from it. R.J.'s goal in writing *Wonder* had been to change how these kids were received socially, and she achieved it. She truly created a movement, the movement of kindness: Kids who had been seen as scary or teased for their differences were being accepted now, more than ever before. And the empathy she inspired wasn't just for our community. Her message was to accept anyone who is different, whether they're transgender, in a wheelchair, autistic, or have Down syndrome or other genetic disorders. She showed that "normal" is everywhere. There are now hundreds of children who like to say, "I'm a real-life *Wonder* kid." And that's a good thing: "We are all *Wonder* people" suits any number of people with differences, including Nathaniel.

My mother told me that at the supermarket where she buys bread, there is always a copy of *Wonder* for sale. That's how far it's reached! Poland isn't a very diverse country, and I can't even think about what it might have been like if Nathaniel had been born in my hometown. People probably would have thought my child was "deformed" because God was punishing me for something like marrying outside of my religion. But *Wonder* opened up a window, and people now have a more scientific understanding of how things like this can happen. Nathaniel hasn't been to Poland yet, but *Wonder* has paved the way for the trip we will take one day.

The 20/20 producers named the hour-long documentary about our family "The Real Wonder Boy," and timed its airing for one day before the movie was released.

When short clips promoting the 20/20 special began appearing, one of the movie producers called Russel, worried. He said, "This show is too real. We want the movie to reach a wide viewership, and we don't want people getting scared."

I was in the kitchen with Russel at the time, and I heard his tone change. In a tight voice, he said, "Hey, dude, what are you talking about, *too real?* This is my life." Then Russel gave him a good five minutes of his opinion. We both knew this producer and were very fond of him. He was a good person, but even someone who had worked so closely with us didn't see that we had no interest in sanitizing our story.

Though I was also miffed, I could understand this producer's point. For a typical 20/20 special, a crew might spend two or three months with their subjects, but they had spent two and a half *years* with our family, covering so many aspects of our lives. For us, the beauty in the special was that Nathaniel's similarities to Auggie became a small part of our story. But for the producer, the promos that said, "It's the real-life Auggie Pullman" made it sound like *Wonder* was based on Nathaniel.

None of us wanted to create that impression. The ads beat the

*Wonder* drum, but *Wonder* is fictional. Our story had started years earlier, and was different. It was ours.

The night the special aired, Russel was with Jacob at a lacrosse tournament, and they watched it in the hotel lobby with his entire team. Nathaniel and I went to a friend's house. I had a knot in my stomach. I had no clue what they would show from the hours of filming they had done. Had it been edited to emphasize the parallels between Auggie and Nathaniel, or toned down because reality was too graphic for the general audience? I ended up loving the way they portrayed our story, evolving from our initial shock and fear of the unknown, through all of the sacrifices, to a moment at the *Wonder* premiere when Nathaniel turns and gives a beautiful smile. It gave me chills.

As things turned out, the combination of the "Real Wonder Boy" documentary and the *Wonder* movie release did lead people to make the connection between Auggie and Nathaniel more than they had before (but not in a bad way, based on the box office numbers). They would come up to Nathaniel and say, "Oh, you're the *Wonder* boy." He would politely correct them: It's not about me; it's about every kid who has a craniofacial condition. But as time passed and Nathaniel healed from the last surgery, people ceased stopping in their tracks when they saw his face. It doesn't seem to make a difference to Nathaniel. He knows who he is, and he still doesn't care what other people think.

# 34. gratitude

When Nathaniel was two weeks old, there was a baby who joined him in the NICU. He had many of the same problems as Nathaniel, plus a cleft lip and palate. The parents didn't speak any English, so there was a translator helping them navigate the complicated medical planet onto which they'd just been teleported. The baby got a trach and a g-tube immediately, and his mom came to visit every day.

Over the years, until the boys were nine or ten years old, I'd cross paths with this family when we had appointments at NYU. The boy had many of the same surgeries as Nathaniel, but his were covered by Medicaid because his parents had little or no income. Each time we saw them, they had more children in tow. They had the babies, a translator, and the surgeries, which they didn't have to pay for. Meanwhile we ended up living in a basement because we couldn't afford the medical bills.

Early on, this didn't seem right to me. I was so mad that I found a phone number online and called the Bush administration's Department of Health and Human Services! Using a dictionary, I wrote out what I was going to say, and when someone answered, I recited, "It's unfair that some people with Medicaid get care for free. My husband was born in this country, and we can't afford a simple apartment. We are living like refugees, in a basement, and these people are getting a free ride." At the time, that was all I could see.

The woman on the other end of the line listened politely, then said, "I'll get word to Mr. President."

I'm not proud that I made that call. Over the years, my view changed. When I look back, I see that no matter what bad luck we were having, Russel always managed to land a better job. When we couldn't afford an apartment, we had generous relatives who took us in, and we had friends and colleagues who gathered together to play golf as a way to raise money for Nathaniel's expenses, and assistance from myFace. We had the education and resources to stay on our feet, move forward when we could, and make our lives better little by little.

This other family, however, had all of our troubles but none of that support, none of those opportunities. Some people aren't given the same chances in life. Take my parents: They weren't lazy or stupid—their options were limited. And I learned so much from my mother, a simple woman who never graduated from college. Now, when I look back, I thank God this family was able to get what they needed. Just because I didn't get the same things didn't mean they shouldn't have them.

When I see immigrants, I know that they came here for a better life. I moved to this country to marry the man I love, so why shouldn't other people be able to find the same happiness? Who am I to judge who is worthy to thrive in America? Now, after all these years, I want everyone to get the help they need. I worry about what would happen to a child with Treacher Collins without any resources, either personally or from the government. If someone needs our help, they should get it, no questions asked.

After years of moving around the country chasing jobs and doctors, we have settled in Seattle, where I teach exercise classes, work at Lululemon, and take our four dogs for long outings at the dog park. (We got Coda, our fourth, during my cancer treatment. I wanted to have two male dogs and two females. For balance, of course.) In our backyard, there are wild rabbits that burrow in the lawn and drive the dogs mad. I love mowing the lawn, and I know where to be careful because the rabbits might be hiding. I know exactly how that mama rabbit feels, safely tucked under the warm earth, biding her time until her babies are strong enough to emerge into the light.

For the first time, Nathaniel is taking after-school classes. He tried tae kwon do when he was little, but he had to wear a helmet, and to do that, he had to take off his hearing aid, and with his hearing aid off, the class was hard to follow. Now he and Jacob are taking tae kwon do together. It's a hard-core class, but he looks forward to it. He says he never realized how hard it is to do a push-up. At home, he practices the combinations of moves, and is dreaming of getting his black belt and becoming a spy. I sit and watch the classes, not because I am worried that he'll get hurt (though I will be nervous when he gets to sparring!), but because, and I hope he'll let me say this, watching him is like Comedy Central.

The boys have also started Hebrew school to prepare for their bar mitzvahs, but when we sat down with Nathaniel to talk about the time and effort that was involved, he got very upset. He said, "It's so much work and time, and I don't even know if I believe in God! If there's a God, why would I have Treacher Collins?" I was surprised. Nathaniel had never talked about God before; he'd never asked why God gave him Treacher Collins. He just did what needed to be done.

In our family, we didn't really talk about God outside of when we were in temple. Getting older means questioning our lives. Asking "why me?" is a part of growing up, and to be Jewish is to ask questions. To have him ask us this seemed normal, but I can't help thinking that his hesitation is also about the time commitment. It's much more appealing to play video games than to learn to read the Torah. For Nathaniel, questioning God went hand-in-hand with being too lazy for Hebrew school.

Jacob is an amazing lacrosse player; Nathaniel entertains himself by imagining stories. Jacob loves movement; Nathaniel loves stillness. For a long time, we urged Nathaniel to support his brother by going to one of his games, but he always protested, "No, this is the biggest punishment you could give me. They just run around the field with those stupid sticks. It's the most boring thing I could imagine, and if I come, I'm bringing my iPad."

Russel said no to the iPad. Jacob said, "It would mean a lot to me if you came. I do stuff to support you."

Finally, one Saturday, Nathaniel said, "I'm coming to Jacob's game today, Mom." Then he winked at me.

I was thinking, *Wow, what changed?*

Later, at the game, he told me, "Dad's going to give me $50 if I watch the game and cheer." Bribery—a parent's last lifeline. Nathaniel set himself up on a chair and yelled, "Hustle, Jacob!" Jacob plays goalie. There was nobody remotely near him, but Nathaniel kept shouting, "Jacob, you got this! Hustle!" Then he turned to me and said, "The more I scream, the sooner I get paid."

For Nathaniel to breathe independently was a massive, years-long medical accomplishment. It was also, on no smaller scale, a triumph of strength and will for a very young boy. Nathaniel will continue to grow and broaden his independence. For instance, I want him to learn how to take care of his hearing aid. It was a relatively small concern before, but now that we've conquered so many other challenges, it's moved to the forefront. I also want him to clean his room. It doesn't feel any bigger than that.

His medical journey isn't over. The bone structure of his face doesn't grow with the rest of his body, and his jaw will just stay where it is. He'll have one more jaw distraction when he stops growing, probably when he's about eighteen, and he'll need a couple of procedures to keep his airway open. We'll try giving him implants around his eyes again. And he desperately needs some dental work.

And then there's his ears, or lack thereof. Russel and I laugh because it seems like having plastic surgery to create nonfunctioning ears is important to a lot of parents of children with Treacher Collins, but it's the last thing on our list. Nathaniel says he doesn't want them, so unless that changes, we won't do it. None of the surgeries he had were for cosmetic reasons, for the purpose of making him look "normal." I support people who undergo surgeries to correct facial differences, but I also want to show what it looks like to love how you look, no matter what. I want it to be normal to be different and proud.

Recently, Russel took Nathaniel in for a follow-up appointment with Dr. Hopper. He called afterward to say, "Dr. Hopper said he'd like to see us in a year."

A year. Just two summers ago, Nathaniel was going to a doctor almost every day. For us, a year feels like a lifetime.

A day later I went to see my new oncologist, Dr. Smith. Sadly, Dr. Press had lost his battle with a brain tumor, and I grieved him as one can only grieve the person who saved your life. At Dr. Smith's office, I spent four hours going from one floor to another, having various tests done. At the end of all of that, Dr. Smith showed me a preliminary report. He explained, "This is a miracle. Your blood doesn't show signs that you had cancer or chemo. You are the healthiest person I've ever seen. Keep doing whatever you're doing."

Then, unbelievably, he said, "I don't want to see you for another year." The exact same words that Nathaniel's doctor had spoken. Two clean bills of health.

The attention I used to give Nathaniel was physical, cleaning him and taking care of his medical needs. Now that I'm done with that, he still gets my full attention, especially on the commute to tae kwon do, when he talks to me about video game characters — a lot. But he also tells me about his dreams of being a veterinarian. He wants us to have a business together: He'll be the vet and I'll be the groomer. He's convinced it's going to happen. Either that, or he'll be a spy; you know, because there's so much overlap in those sets of skills.

Jacob has his own transition to make. Looking out for Nathaniel, being responsible for his brother's well-being has been part of his life, just like being born with Treacher Collins is part of Nathaniel's. Between his brother's surgeries and my cancer, Jacob grew up accustomed to worrying, which is a habit that doesn't disappear overnight. He's still haunted, even by minor things, and when he gets stressed out about a test or some everyday issue, he has flashbacks to the scariest moments with me and Nathaniel. In a way, it's his turn to process. As he says, "I'm a bit scarred. But, like Nathaniel's scars, mine give me character." Unlike Nathaniel, Jacob wants to live far away from us when he grows up, in North Carolina or San Diego. He wants to be an oncologist researching a cure for cancer.

I used to have anxiety every day. My chest always hurt, a weird pinching pain. I was so emotionally and physically exhausted that I couldn't get myself up and about, so I'd lie in bed, something I considered to be a "bad" thing that I did. It wasn't necessarily depression, I was just overwhelmed. Or maybe my body was tired from the chemo, but for a while there I'd lie down whenever I could.

It took me the first eight to ten years of Nathaniel's life to overcome that constant state of panic. I had to retrain my brain. I don't nap as much as I used to, but the best way for me to relax and restore myself is still to crawl in bed, surround myself with animals, and shut down my brain. Sometimes I ask my kids what heaven would be for them, if heaven is a moment in which you would happily live for the rest of forever. Jacob says that for him, heaven is being on the lacrosse field with his teammates. For Nathaniel, it's being in his room, playing with Legos, with the dogs watching him.

My heaven is taking a nap surrounded by the beating hearts of the dogs: Snowball on my head, Brownie and Smokey next to my thighs, and Coda next to my heart.

Russel and I married young, started our family right away, and immediately entered a parallel universe where everything was foreign and scary. We were in survival mode for so long. How did we find time to love each other and be a married couple? I never thought about our relationship. The only thing I was thinking was, *How can we be there for this fragile, sick baby?* The thought of talking about us or even fighting didn't cross my mind. And all the love I showed was through Nathaniel. We were caring for him together and giving him the best life we could.

That was my marriage: our shared sense of love and duty. I couldn't have done it without Russel, and my love for him swelled when I saw how gentle and calm he was, and how much strength he had in stressful situations. He literally saved Nathaniel's life many times. He had his moments—we both did—but I saw him as a superman. After sleepless nights caring for our son, he'd go to work exhausted but determined to provide for us. Nathaniel, and later Jacob, were our bond—they kept us both sane and together.

Russel brings me coffee in bed and lets me sleep late. I cook his meals, do his laundry, and take care of our kids. We show love by the silent choices we make. We don't go on dates; we're happier when the kids are with us. Even if we do go out together alone—and we have tried more than once—all we do is talk about the boys and how much we miss them. So instead, we go to spin class together, grab a juice, or watch a movie. How did we find time to love each other and be married? I don't know the answer to that, except that we had to each love the other one for the sacrifices they made.

Lately, we have gravitated to a new nightly routine. We sit together on the couch and watch each other's favorite shows. For Russel, that's *Iron Chef* and *Beat Bobby Flay*, and for me, it's *House Hunters*. He sits in his spot with Smokey, and I'm with the other three dogs. We're like old people, having a glass of wine and savoring our well-earned leisure.

*Nathaniel: The surgeries haven't affected me all that much mentally. I guess I handle pain better and differently, so that makes some things easier. Mostly, I avoid talking about my medical experiences. It's not because talking brings back any kind of trauma. But my surgeries already took up so much of my time and they all blend together, so I don't have very many specific memories, or much to say about the annoying need to be fixed. I'm definitely an expert on what it's like being in a hospital and how a basic surgery goes. My recent big surgeries are still fresh in my mind, but the ones before that have faded and jumbled together. Chances are that by the time I'm thirty or so, things like doctors, hospitals, and infections will all be in the past, and the memories will be even smaller and more insignificant.*

*Our family has gone through more than most people, but we're a "normal" family now. Or maybe we used to be a normal family under extraordinary circumstances and now we're a normal family under normal circumstances. I don't think we're extraordinary people, except maybe my mom, because she did so much of the worrying and had to deal with medical stuff that really grossed her out. Either way, who I am will never change. Treacher Collins doesn't define me. What defines all of us is how we face what we've been given. I'm Nathaniel. I'm not normal, and neither are you.*

I played piano for my entire youth, for many hours, every day, until I moved to America. When Nathaniel was born, he became the center of my world and I left piano behind. I don't miss it, but I *am* glad for what I took from it: commitment, striving for excellence, appreciating art and beauty. We've often said that Nathaniel spent enough time at doctors, in the hospital, and recovering to become a concert pianist. But I was a concert pianist and look where it got me! My point is that something that seems central to your world can easily be eclipsed by time and chance. Nathaniel is right: His trach and all that went with it will recede into the past, but he is stronger for all those experiences and that strength will serve him forever.

When Nathaniel used to check in at New York hospitals, the nurse always checked his vitals and went through a list of questions to make sure he was healthy enough for surgery. When he got to be a certain age, they added a series of questions about his home life, things like: Is anyone touching you inappropriately at home? At school? Do you ever think about suicide? They ask the parents to step out of the room so the child has a chance to report abuse.

When Nathaniel was eight or nine, the nurse came out of the prep room crying.

"What did he do? What happened?" I asked, understandably concerned.

The nurse, who knew what we'd been through, said, "When I asked him if he'd ever thought about hurting himself, he said, 'That might be the stupidest question I've heard in my life.' So I asked what he meant by that and he replied, 'I have the greatest life ever. I have an awesome mom and dad and brother. I have a dog named Smokey. Why would I hurt myself? My life is awesome.'"

For the first thirteen years of Nathaniel's life, I longed for the elusive state of what I thought was normal, whatever that was. For us, it never had to do with what anyone else wanted or expected of us, but there was a freedom that I saw in the people around us. I wanted that for our whole family. In a way we achieved that freedom when Nathaniel got rid of his trach. But even if that hadn't been an option or a success, we would have continued to strive for the best possible lives, to find peace in every day, and to thank God for what we were given.

# afterword:
# swimming like a fish

Russel took Nathaniel to San Diego for his eighth-grade spring break. He's taken lots of trips with Jacob, mostly for sports, and he wanted to take Nathaniel on a vacation that didn't have anything to do with doctors' appointments. They went to SeaWorld, where you can swim with the dolphins, and at the end of the first day, they Skyped me to report back.

Russel said, "We beat this thing—we got through it. He's breathing on his own! The horrible halo, everything, it was all worth it."

Nathaniel chimed in, "It was awesome!"

Russel laughed. "The minute it was over, this guy wanted to ride the roller coaster. It was a lot more emotional and rewarding for me than it was for him."

We always had doubts: Should we put him through this? Did we push too hard? Was it worth the risk? Swimming with the dolphins was something we had only dreamed Nathaniel would be able to do someday. This was true validation that we had made the right choices. Our son was on a dolphin's back, alive and thriving. He refused to define himself by what he'd been through.

*Nathaniel: We walked in water up to our chests out to the middle of a large pool. We were standing on a ledge, and the water on both sides of us was a lot deeper, maybe thirty feet, the way the dolphins like it. The trainers lined us up and, on cue, a dolphin swam up to each of us. We gave them commands and fed them fish when they responded. Then we were each told to put our arms around a dolphin, and they carried us across the pool. It was a fast ride, maybe a few seconds, though it probably wasn't the dolphin's full speed. It was amazing to be among those animals—you could tell that they were as smart as humans. It was nothing they did—you could just feel it.*

*I couldn't have gone into water that deep, with splashy animals like that, when I had a trach. But I don't plan to go through my life saying, "I couldn't do this before and now I can." That would be kind of the opposite of getting upset about the things you can't do, and I don't do that either. I'm more an in-the-moment kind of guy.*

On Fridays, the boys join Russel and me in front of the TV for movie night. The kids give me a list of the candy they want me to buy, we make popcorn (one of the only smells Nathaniel can identify is butter), and we sit together in our tiny front room, covered in blankets and dogs, always in the same spots. Nathaniel has a big, round chair that he drags in from the playroom. Jacob pulls in a smaller black chair and, because he's closest to the ground, the dogs are always after his popcorn. He whispers, "You had enough! You had enough!"

Smokey sits with Russel and watches intently, waiting for an animal to come on screen; I learned from Smokey that almost every movie has an animal in it. When one finally appears, he starts growling. He's a movie talker—Nathaniel can't stand it because his hearing aid makes it hard for him to separate the sounds from the movie and other noise. Russel is in charge of keeping Smokey's enthusiasm under control, but truth is, I'm a far worse movie talker than Smokey. "I can't believe that happened!" I'll say. "Oh my gosh!"

Nathaniel will reprimand me. "Shhhh, Mom! This is why I don't like to go out to the movies — because of people like you."

The dogs dive between us to score dropped popcorn kernels. Russel brings me an extra blanket. Everyone's together and it's just great.

# acknowledgments

There are so many people to thank that I simply can't thank each of you individually. You know who you are, and if you don't see your name on these pages, please know that I didn't forget you and I love you.

First of all, I would like to thank Hilary Liftin, my amazing collaborator. Without you, this book simply would not exist. Thank you from the bottom of my heart for listening so patiently to all of the stories that took place in my life and placing them so brilliantly into the pages of this book. Thank you for your wise advice and humor that made some of the "heavy" subjects more bearable. I am forever grateful for our friendship, not only on a professional level. You have taught me so much about having my own voice and truly listening to everyone with an open mind.

I would like to thank my husband, Russel. I am not an easy person to be married to and the fact that you are still around means that you truly love me. I love you dearly and appreciate everything you have done for our family. You always found the way to look forward with a smile, despite many dark moments that filled our path. Our children are lucky to have you as their dad because you have taught them not only how to love and care, but also how to be responsible for their own actions and respectful to others.

Many thanks to my amazing sons, Nathaniel and Jacob. You are the reason that I am alive. You both keep me going, you put a smile on my face, and you always remind me how lucky I am to have you as my children.

I would like to thank Daniel Greenberg, my literary agent. Thank you for representing me and my story in the publishing world. I will never forget the first journey you took me on in NYC to introduce me to publishers. I got to see a beautiful and kind world of literature, how much happens "behind the scenes," and how many people are involved. I loved exploring this world with you and will never forget our adventure. Thank you for all of your effort to bring this story to life. Thanks to Tim Wojcik at Levine Greenberg Literary Agency for picking up the phone when I called and connecting me to Daniel, and for all his work afterward.

I would like to thank Deb Brody and Jamie Selzer, our amazing editors. Thank you for taking the time and giving us such constructive feedback in the editing process. Because of your hard and thorough work, this book has a shape and form that makes total sense.

Thank you to all of the doctors across the country who took care of my health needs, especially Drs. Alfred Newman, Larry Mogul, and Oliver Press. I owe my life to you. Because of your medical expertise and hope, I am still on this earth and able to share my story.

Thanks to Dr. Joseph McCarthy. I will never forget what you told me about allowing Nathaniel to be a kid, that you could fix a broken arm but not his psyche. I took those wise words to heart and used them as my mantra in the early years of Nathaniel's childhood. Thank you for all you did for Nathaniel. Your pioneering medical procedures not only changed my son's life but are changing and improving many lives right now.

Thank you to Dr. Joseph Bernstein and Dr. Kaalan Johnson.

We could not have dreamed of more caring and loving ENTs. Thank you for not giving up on Nathaniel and always giving us hope. Because of that hope and your amazing surgical skills, Nathaniel is finally trach-free.

Thank you to Dr. Richard Hopper. Your game-changing, pioneering procedure has made our dreams for Nathaniel a reality.

Thank you to the wonderful army of nurses from various hospitals across the country. Your love and care always brightened our days. Many of those days were dark and filled with fear and tears, and because of your smiles and positivity we were able to keep going.

Thank you to Pat Chibbaro and Shelley Cohen from NYU Medical Center. I will never forget how much hope you gave me. You became my family away from home in the early days of Nathaniel's life. I will never forget your friendship, love, and support.

Thank you to my family in Poland. You are always here for me, willing to listen, cry, and laugh with me. Thank you for your unconditional love. I am always looking forward to our next national park adventure.

Finally, I would like to thank R.J. Palacio. Many years ago, when we first met, you planted the seed of desire in me to write a book one day. The idea was brewing for quite some time, and finally the book is here. Thank you for introducing me to Daniel Greenberg and Jim Levine. I am truly grateful for all of your support. And thank you for writing *Wonder*. Your little blue book not only made life for children like my son much easier, but will have a tremendous impact on generations to come. You have taught so many children to accept differences and how to be kind to each other. I can't wait for them to grow up and lead us all.